BLESS THE LORD ON THE JOURNEY

Dr. Patrick Pang

Unless otherwise indicated, Scripture quotations used in this book are from:

The Amplified Bible (AMP) 2015 by Zondervan and The Lockman Foundation. Used by permission.

Other Scripture quotations are from the following sources:

New American Standard Bible (NASB) 1960, 1962, 1963, 1971, 1973, 1975, and 1977 by The Lockman Foundation. Used by permission.

The New International Version of the Bible (NIV), 1984 by the International Bible Society. Used by permission of Zondervan Bible Publishers.

The New Living Translation (NLT) 2008 by Tyndale House Publishers. Used by permission.

Revised Standard Version (RSV), 1952, 1971 by the National Council of the Churches of Christ. Used by permission.

The New King James Version (NKJV), copyright 1979, 1980, 1982, 1984 Thomas Nelson, Inc., Publisher. Used by permission.

King James Version (KJV).

Book Cover & Design by: Karen Brock

ISBN: 979—8-9855618-1-4

Printed in the United States of America

DEDICATION

I gratefully and affectionately dedicate this book to Rose,
who continues to cause my heart to flutter.
From the rising of the sun to the setting of the same,
I cannot adequately thank God that you have chosen
to share this ministry journey of faith together with me.

ENDORSEMENTS

This inspiring book is both a classroom and a chapel – it teaches and instructs us, but at the same time carries such a devotional tone too. Through scripture insights and powerful quotations from those who have gone before us, Patrick walks us through many different aspects of the Christian journey, encouraging us to bless the Lord with every step. Enjoy!

MATT REDMAN,
GRAMMY AWARD-WINNING WORSHIP LEADER,
SINGER, SONGWRITER & AUTHOR.

Patrick's ability to tell personal stories that are woven skillfully with the Word of God is like few people I've ever met. This man knows his Bible and he lives his life by it. Be prepared to dive deep and to be challenged by *Bless the Lord on the Journey* as you see him take the Word of God and explain it in a way that you can't help but see the application to your own life.

Patrick embodies the passage in Nehemiah: "They read from the book, from the Law of God, translating to give the sense so that they understood the reading" (Nehemiah 8:8, NASB).

On top of his understanding of the Word of God, Patrick's knowledge of history, and his love of many of the great hymns and choruses of the faith come out strongly as he weaves his way through each chapter. It's obvious what a significant role the music of our faith plays in Patrick's life.

Read this book and here is a word to the wise … changes in your life may be taking place soon.

DOUG BRIDGES,
OWNER AND CEO,
WEST COAST FIRE AND WATER.

This book is akin to a 3-in-1 product. By reading this book one can gain insights from the journeys of three groups of individuals in human history; characters from the Old Testament including Abraham, Moses, Joseph, David, among others; and Paul, Peter, Mary Magdelene, Lazarus and Jesus from the New Testament. Finally, the personal journeys of Patrick and his beloved wife Rose are illustrated.

My friend Patrick has exquisitely blended the journeys of each of the characters mentioned above to bring out important traits in Christian character development, and pitfalls to avoid. They inspire, encourage, and in certain chapters admonish the reader to live out the life God intends for each of us and thus help us recalibrate our lives as we read the journeys of each character featured in this book.

I have known Patrick for over half a century. I can vouch for his devotion to his God, his wife Rose, and his dedication to ministry. He has first-hand experience of the faithfulness of God upon his life. Many of the chapters detail his own journey as he candidly shares them to encourage and to remind us of what a great God we have. He writes: "If God has provided for Rose and me in almost fifty years, He will provide for you. If God has opened doors to over one thousand churches in Anglo, Black, Hispanic, and Asian communities for us across the United States of America, surely, He can do the same for you. The question is: Do you trust Him to do it for you?" Patrick concludes: "You will ride through some dark valleys, but because He is with you, you will soar among the stars." And to that, I say, "Amen!"

This is not a book about theology. It is, more importantly, a book that translates theology into various guideposts to aid the readers to live life to the fullest as they navigate their own journey. *Bless the Lord on the Journey* aptly reminds us that we are all sojourners in this world but we are not alone, for "He is there and He is not silent." As we journey together, may our faith in Jesus strengthen.

It is with much delight and honor that I recommend this book to you, a book whose breadth and scope will provide much for introspection and reflection.

DEACON DANIEL SOH,
CHAIRMAN, BAPTIST THEOLOGICAL SEMINARY,
SINGAPORE,
PAST PRESIDENT, QUEENSTOWN BAPTIST CHURCH,
SINGAPORE.

I was enormously encouraged and touched by what Dr. Pang shared in his book, *Bless the Lord on the Journey.* Through his personal experiences, scripture illustrations and references to hymns, we can see the powerful testimonies of God's grace at work. It was uplifting reading the book and invited me to rejoice and reflect on my own journey with the Lord. As you delve deeply into this book, you will also enjoy your journey with the Lord and be blessed.

DR. LI YUNG HUA,
ORTHOPAEDIC AND SPINE SURGEON,
ORTHOPAEDIC ASSOCIATES, SINGAPORE.

Following along in the same vein as his previous book *Faith Journey*, Dr. Pang has written another book, *Bless the Lord on the Journey,* comprising of forty short chapters that are great for devotional reading.

Like a tapestry, Patrick has intricately interwoven the ups and downs in the experience of his own life journey with quotations from many great spiritual men and women, past and present.

After reading this book, I am reminded that "since we also have such a great cloud of witnesses surrounding us, let's rid ourselves of every obstacle and the sin which so easily entangles us, and let's run with endurance the race that is set before us, looking only at Jesus, the originator and perfecter of the faith, who for the joy set before Him endured the cross, despising the shame, and has sat down at the right hand of the throne of God" (Hebrews 12:1-2, NASB).

Furthermore, he has layered in many relevant passages from the Word of God to suggest that our stories should be deeply intertwined into His Story. We are to find the meaning of our own story only in the light of the greater Narrative. Read the book and enjoy the journey!

DR. CHI WEI MING,
GENERAL PRACTITIONER,
SIMS DRIVE MEDICAL CLINIC, SINGAPORE.
PAST CHAIRMAN, WYCLIFFE SINGAPORE,

Each one of us finds ourselves on a journey. Patrick has strategically filled these pages with spiritual wisdom and timeless truths that will encourage and equip us as the sons and daughters of God. If taken to heart and placed into practice, these foundational keys will open the doors of faithfulness, perseverance and eternal impact on this journey that has been set before us.

REV. KRIS STRICKLAND,
SENIOR PASTOR, COAST CHRISTIAN CENTER.

In his latest book, Pastor Pang outlines important considerations for all who desire God's direction in their life journey. Each chapter in *Bless the Lord on the Journey* is filled with relevant and insightful scripture that keeps the reader engaged. His poignant references from renowned Christian speakers and key quotes from respected leaders help validate each chapter. You'll recognize and relate to many beloved hymns and song lyrics as well as select poetry we are reminded of by Dr. Pang.

This book is an impressive collection of Patrick's lifetime study of the Lord's desire for our lives. Whether you are an emerging Christian leader or a layperson, you will find this book to be a comprehensive and insightful read as you consider your own personal journey.

We found it to be a blessing!

REBBECCA & BILL EVANS,
CO-FOUNDERS AVE13 LLC,
MARY KAY SR. NATIONAL DIRECTOR EMERITUS.

Dr. Patrick Pang has laid out a thoughtful plan for following God through the thick and thin of ministry leading to a productive and successful life of Christian service. *Bless the Lord on the Journey*, has a nuts-and-bolts approach that allows the reader searching for the right ministry tool to locate the subject that will bring new insight.

I commend Pastor Patrick's insightful writing to those who wish to understand the challenges of ministry and God's provision for all who are seeking to serve our Lord Jesus Christ in vocational Christian ministry.

RICHARD OWEN,
PAST MODERATOR, PURPOSE CHURCH.

After fifty fruitful years in the Christian ministry, Dr. Patrick Pang has laid out a perfect and inspiring blueprint for ministry work. Whether you are serving God as a pastor or a parishioner, a ministry leader or a lay person, *Bless the Lord on the Journey* is a must read. It is absolutely spot on.

As you read Dr. Pang's book, I pray that you will bless the Lord on your journey as well.

RON SALISBURY,
OWNER, PRESIDENT & CEO,
ABC PEST CONTROL.

"When setting out on a journey, do not seek advice from someone who has never left home." Wise words, purportedly from the 13th century Persian poet Rumi.

The author of this book, Dr Patrick Pang, early in life departed from these shores in pursuit of God's will for his life. And now he documents his experience and learning for the benefit of others … his signature tune.

He draws from quotations, lyrics and true-life illustrations for a heady brew of thoughts, ideas, suggestions and advice, nudging us to pursue the road which is difficult and only found by a few, but we must go: "where strait is the gate and narrow is the way" (Matthew 7:14, KJV). It's more a Path than an Expressway.

We recognize that for any Journey, the Destination is important. That makes the trip worthwhile and meaningful. Indeed, even valuable. But the Journey is not a Race. Pacing oneself with one's escort-mentor is paramount, as Dr Pang learned. This book becomes his thanksgiving offering to the Lord Jesus Christ for accompanying him through his earthly sojourn. Like all journeys, there are roadblocks, diversions, slippery slopes, unexpected encounters aplenty. Help is at hand with God's presence and power.

The words of C. S. Lewis echo in our hearts: "You can't go back and change the beginning but you can start where you are and change the ending." Exactly. The journey awaits. Get a head start and get going. You'll be glad you did.

DR. ANDREW GOH,
EDITOR, IMPACT MAGAZINE,
FOUNDING ELDER, RIVERLIFE CHURCH, SINGAPORE.

Dr. Patrick Pang has been living this book since the day he decided to follow Jesus many years ago. His endless zeal for Jesus and the Gospel is equally matched by his tireless and persistent pursuit of doing the will of God. I and my wife, Maria, have known Dr. Pang for many years and have been enormously encouraged and exhorted by his dynamic messages and faithful life. I count it as an honor to have him as my friend. I am confident you will likewise be encouraged along your journey as you read and consider the words penned by Dr. Pang.

AARON D. WATSON,
ELDER, COAST CHRISTIAN CENTER.

In *Bless the Lord on the Journey*, Dr. Patrick Pang shares how God first spoke to his heart as a young man, then guided, provided, sustained, nourished, and walked with him and his wife Rose in ministry over the next fifty years.

This engaging book provides insight and wisdom gained from a personal relationship with Jesus Christ as Lord and Savior. Solidly grounded in Scripture and digging deep into topics with unparalleled research, Dr. Pang uses a plethora of traditional, contemporary, and historic hymns, songs, and worship music; quotes from well-known pastors and preachers (past and present) along with artists, poets, authors, politicians, and early Christian "fathers" of the faith, to enhance, pique our interest, and fill us with God's living Word.

Forty chapters, focusing on essentials of the journey, give the readers pause for reflection, enrich our understanding, and point us to Jesus Christ, "the author (originator) and finisher (perfector) of our faith" (Hebrews 12:2, NASB). Patrick's journey, and certainly our own, includes struggles, triumphs, testing, failures, doubts, suffering, loss, emotions, waiting, uncertainties, prayer, and faith. Psalm 103:1 exhorts: "Bless the LORD, O my soul and all that is within me, bless His Holy name" (NASB).

Can our lives on this journey with all its twists and turns truly "bless the Lord?" Patrick's heart-felt answer to this question, developed throughout the book, is a resounding "yes!"

Finally, we must expectantly look forward to our destination: a "hope" and "future" guaranteed by God Himself (Jeremiah 29:11). *Bless the Lord on the Journey* is a book not to just read, but to devour, and not just once, but multiple times.

RICK PIERCY,
GRIEFSHARE FACILITATOR,
CALVARY CHAPEL.

ACKNOWLEDGMENTS

Honor that is not expressed is not honor. Someone once said that a philosopher is a person who talks about things he doesn't understand, but he makes it sound like it's your fault. I am not a philosopher!

As I write this book, geopolitical conditions continue to worsen, families continue to weaken, and morals continue to wane. But one constant remains – faithful friends. With gratitude, I want to thank my friends and colleagues in ministry for the earnest efforts of their endorsements.

I want to thank Matt Redman, the Grammy Award-winning worship leader and song writer for his kind endorsement. My book was written while I listened to the soothing strains of his hit song and music: "10,000 Reasons (Bless the Lord)."

Dr. Warren H. Stewart, Sr. has lovingly led the First Institutional Baptist Church in Phoenix, Arizona, as their Senior Pastor for almost fifty years! Pastor Stewart was the first one to invite me to preach at his prestigious pulpit when I received the call to be the Regional Director of Evangelism for the Pacific Southwest in 1987. I thank him for writing the Foreword to this book.

This book could not have been published without our friends who have remained supportive through the years: Doug and Krishelle Bridges – in over fifty years of ministry on two continents, Rose and I have only met one entire family of four generations who is completely sold out to Jesus! Dinah Brooks and Bev Rogers can always be counted on. My friend and brother, Pastor Kris Strickland, has driven seven hours twice a year to pick me up from the San Francisco airport to take me to Fort Bragg and back. He has done it for the last eight years!

I want to thank Karen Brock for her invaluable assistance as my editor. Her discerning eye to detail is appreciated.

As God rejoices over His bride (Isaiah 62:5), so I rejoice over Rose, my bride of forty-six years! Who am I that God has blessed me with a wife who has encouraged me enormously? She knows me well enough to be familiar with all my faults, yet she continues to be thankful for me. She always makes my heart skip a beat. She is the apple of my eye!

No one has impacted me more positively, more profoundly, more permanently, or more personally than Jesus Christ my Lord. That's why the lyrics of blind Fanny J. Crosby continue to echo in my soul today:

> This is my story, this is my song,
> Praising my Savior all the day long.
> This is my story, this is my song,
> Praising my Savior all the day long.

Finally, thank you for reading this book. It is my hope that you will bless the Lord on your journey.

PATRICK PANG,
LOS ANGELES, CALIFORNIA.

FOREWORD

Who does *not* need to bless the Lord along the journeys in life where He leads us? Absolutely no one, at least, that is the vitally important message of this new book, *Bless the Lord on the Journey*, written by my brother, colleague and friend of over three decades, Dr. Patrick Pang. Providentially, it was my privilege to read this inspiring book while my wife and I were leading a mission team of eleven persons on a journey through South Africa, Kenya and Rwanda.

Dr. Pang writes in a unique style that makes each chapter of this book short, succinct and intentional in describing the blessings that come from the Lord as we journey through life. Most beneficial is the fact that Patrick does not just identify the high points of life's journeys. Indeed, he takes time to write about various aspects of our journeys which necessitate caution and care.

In many ways, this is a devotional book to be read over and over again at every leg of our life's journeys as a way to bless the Lord. Dr. Pang uses examples in Scripture to support the focal point of each of his chapters. His wealth of knowledge of great leaders in history who have made their life's journeys complements what he writes in each chapter.

Of course, quite transparently, the author shares powerful bits and pieces of his own personal journey from Singapore to the USA and around the world representing Jesus Christ. The wisdom of being a servant leader in the Body of Christ as a preacher, pastor, husband, father, denominational leader, teacher, missionary and mentor for several decades is revealed in every page of Dr. Pang's book. In particular, he is a well-known, frequent guest preacher and teacher at the First Institutional Baptist Church in Phoenix, Arizona where God has allowed me to serve as senior pastor for almost 50 years.

Take note of the sampling of the diverse subject matter that will enthusiastically engage the reader on his or her journey reading this book—humility, discipline, God's awareness of our human frailty, rejection, faith and doubt, encouragement, grace, sin, failure, forgiveness, restoration and God's presence all along the way. Dr. Pang courageously addresses mountaintop as well as valley experiences of every one of us which are so often hardly ever mentioned in books to inspire and edify.

This invaluable book meets each of us right where God has us in our respective life's transitions from one point to the next. It is virtually guaranteed that the reader will be uplifted and enlightened as he or she journeys through each page of *Bless the Lord on the Journey*.

DR. WARREN H. STEWART, SR.
SR. PASTOR, FIRST INSTITUTIONAL BAPTIST CHURCH,
PHOENIX, ARIZONA.

CONTENTS

INTRODUCTION

I hope you will find this book personal, practical and positive.

God longs to empower us with His permanent presence, comfort us in our struggles and our sorrows, strengthen us in our journey, and revolutionize us in our pilgrimage from this planet to paradise.

This is a book for the heart much more than for the head. I do not intend to discuss or debate the presence of God in these printed pages. Neither do I intend to engage in theological and theoretical minutia. I am acutely aware and completely convinced that there are thrilling things and transformative thoughts hidden in the Scriptures.

Talk about discovering God's Word! Hidden in the Scriptures are priceless verbal vaults awaiting discovery and application.

So come with me as we *Bless the Lord on the Journey.* God intends that we should enjoy the journey as much as the destination. You may live to see the day when your journey is among your most cherished memories.

1.

BLESS THE LORD ON THE JOURNEY

"Life is difficult."[1] The raw reality that Scott Peck introduces in his book is no less true today than when it was first written over forty years ago.

If life is difficult, I can say with complete truthfulness that preaching is a tough task. I have come to this conclusion after fifty years of preaching.

It encourages and excites me when I pick up my pen to write *Bless the Lord on the Journey*. This is the sequel to my first book, *Faith Journey.*[2]

This book you hold in your hands did not emerge from a sole source. Indeed, the credit for this book belongs to the One who came to me before the many winters of my life.

If you find yourself in a dark, damp and distressing dungeon along your journey, you will discover as I have, that the One who comes to you in this season of your life, is still the One who takes you by the hand.

Prayer and Preparation

In fifty years of preaching, I have learned that I must be thoroughly prepared. It takes time to prepare.

Time spent in prayer and preparation for the proclamation of the Word is never wasted. D. A. Carson reminds us that "our low spiritual ebb is directly traceable to the flickering feebleness of our prayers."[3]

Prayer bends our will to God's will. E. Stanley Jones, the renowned missionary explains:

> "If I throw out a boathook from the boat and catch hold of the shore and pull, do I pull the shore to me, or do I pull myself to the shore? Prayer is not pulling God to my will, but the aligning of my will to the will of God."[4]

The day after President Roosevelt's death, Truman met with supporters and said:

> "Boys, if you ever pray, pray for me now. I don't know if you fellas ever had a load of hay fall on you, but when they told me what happened yesterday, I felt like the moon, the stars, and all the planets had fallen on me."[5]

The backbone of any work done for God is prayer. John Henry Newman, a nineteenth-century English scholar and churchman, writes:

> "Prayer is to the spiritual life what the beating of the pulse and the drawing of the breath are to the life of the body."[6]

Aaron and Hur were called to assist Moses, sitting him on a stone and standing at his side to hold his hands heavenward. When sunset came, Moses' hands were still reaching upward to God, and Israel had carried the day. Forever fixed in Joshua's mind was the image of Aaron and Hur coming to Moses' side and lifting his hands up to God (Exodus 17:8-13). E. M. Bounds clearly communicates:

> "They are not leaders because of brilliancy … but because, by the power of prayer, they could command the power of God."[7]

John Henry Jowett, a powerful preacher of yesteryear, notes that "Preaching that costs nothing accomplishes nothing." [8] In preparing to preach, sometimes the emotions of my heart cloud the expressions of my mouth. That's why I admire and appreciate the lyrics of Matt Redman, the Grammy Award-winning worship leader, singer-songwriter and author:

> Bless the Lord, O my soul,
> O my soul, worship His holy Name,
> Sing like never before, O my soul,
> I'll worship Your holy Name.
>
> The sun comes up, it's a new day dawning;
> It's time to sing Your song again.
> Whatever may pass and whatever lies before me,
> Let me be singing when the evening comes.

You're rich in love and You're slow to anger,
Your name is great and Your heart is kind;
For all Your goodness I will keep on singing,
Ten thousand reasons for my heart to find.

Bless the Lord, O my soul,
O my soul, worship His holy Name,
Sing like never before, O my soul,
I'll worship Your holy Name.[9]

Psalms

I believe it was Martin Luther who says that: "Next to the Word of God, music deserves the highest praise."[10] Even Nietzche, whose worldview was predominantly dark and cynical, says that "without music, human life would be a mistake."[11] The longest of the sixty-six books in the Bible is the one dedicated to the hymns of the Hebrews.

I cannot tell you how frequently my wife, Rose, and I have returned to the Psalms where that tender and talented musician composed melodies that prompted us to worship God. They not only give us fresh faith but also high hopes to press on.

The great Baptist preacher, Charles Haddon Spurgeon writes: "The delightful study of the Psalms has yielded me boundless profit and ever-growing pleasure."[12] This is not a superficial statement.

Those who would grow spiritually spend hours in the Psalms for times of refreshment and recovery. No wonder the peerless pastor G. Campbell Morgan says:

"The Book of Psalms ... is the book in which the emotions of the human soul find expression ... Are you glad? I can find you a Psalm that you can sing. Are you sad? I can find you a Psalm that will suit that occasion ... The Psalms range over the whole gamut of human emotions."[13]

Psalm 103

Psalm 103 inspired Matt Redman to write this melodious song – "10,000 Reasons (Bless the Lord)."[14] In the last few years, before I write a message or a presentation, I would listen to the soothing strains of this song.

True worship flows from the inside out. Worship is not an external activity, but it is of necessity first internal. That's why Saint Augustine says it best: "A Christian should be an alleluia from head to foot."[15]

Psalm 103 is David's "Hallelujah Chorus."[16] It is a psalm of breathtaking beauty. There are twenty-two verses, just as there are twenty-two letters in the Hebrew alphabet. It is called an envelope psalm because it commences and concludes in the same way with the same words: "Bless the LORD, O my soul!" (Psalm 103:1, 22, ESV).

The psalmist prescribes his worship experience of an august and awesome God in these sublime sentences:

"Bless the LORD, O my soul, and all that is within me,
Bless his holy name!
Bless the LORD, O my soul,
And forget not all his benefits,
who forgives all your iniquity,
who heals all your diseases,

who redeems your life from the pit,
who crowns you with steadfast love and mercy,
who satisfies you with good
so that your youth is renewed like the eagle's" (Psalm 103:1-5, ESV).

Jesus' sure statement in John 4:23 that the Father seeks worshipers is unparalleled, for nowhere in the verbal vault of Scripture do we read that God seeks anything else from a child of God.[17] God desires worship more than anything else.

Thus, every Christ-follower must understand that worship is our ultimate priority. Worship is what God wants from you and me. Thomas à Kempis used this prayer of submission: "As Thou wilt; what Thou wilt; when Thou wilt."[18]

We must come with great expectation – for we will experience just what we expect. Martin Luther eloquently expresses that "a fire is kindled in my heart, and it breaks its way through."[19]

Psalm 103 is a psalm of perfect praise. God's great grace parades before the sweet singer of Israel. David "soars on wings like eagles" (Isaiah 40:31, NIV) when he thinks of God:

"Bless the LORD, O my soul, and all that is within me,
Bless his holy name!
Bless the LORD, O my soul,
And forget not all his benefits" (Psalm 103:1-2, ESV).

Even though David mentions five attributes for which the believer can offer praise to God (Psalm 103:1-5), Matt Redman calls his song "10,000 Reasons (Bless the Lord)."[20]

First, God "forgives all your iniquity" (Psalm 103:3, ESV). This is something to praise God for! God, who has every reason to judge us for our iniquities, graciously grants us His mercy. We need to convince the world that our God forgives not just once or twice, but repeatedly. He forgives not just so-called little sins but also the supremely shameful and significant ones. From the Psalms, we are acutely aware of our own failures and our own need for forgiveness. God "is compassionate and gracious, slow to anger, and abounding in love" (Psalm 103:8, NIV). That's why Redman sings,

> You're rich in love and You're slow to anger,
> Your name is great and Your heart is kind;[21]

Satan is known as "the accuser of the brethren" (Revelation 12:10, KJV). Because he is invisible, he is all the more insidious. He tells lies about us. What Sissela Bok says is instructive and insightful: "It is easy for the devil to tell a lie but hard for the devil to tell only one."[22]

What happens when Satan arrives in God's presence as our accuser? He is stopped at once. He comes as our adversary (1 Peter 5:8, RSV), but there stands our Advocate, Jesus Christ the righteous (1 John 2:2, KJV).

This is what God has done with our sins. He has taken them away and placed them on Jesus. He has taken them away and put them in the sea of God's forgetfulness.

Second, God "heals all your diseases" (Psalm 103:3, ESV). This verse does not refer to the healing of the body, but to the healing of the soul. This is clear from the grammatical construction of the sentence. In this verse the pronoun "your" stands for the noun "soul." So what is David saying? He is saying, "Bless the LORD, O my soul … who heals all your [soul's] diseases."

The soul does indeed have its diseases, just like the body. In the wise words of Charles Kemp:

> "Every need known to man is described in the Bible … the jealousy of Saul, the loyalty of Jonathan, the courage of Nathan, the despair of Jeremiah, and the struggles of Paul … in the Scriptures are portrayed the results of such crippling emotions like guilt, doubt, futility, and fear, which warp and twist a life and disturb and destroy the soul."[23]

The Word of God is "alive and active. Sharper than any double-edged sword, it penetrates even to dividing soul and spirit" (Hebrews 4:12, NIV). It slices even as it comforts the afflicted and afflicts the comfortable. The purpose of preaching is to relate the sharp sword of the Word of God to the needs of women and men. If I am going to address those needs, I must know the hopes and fears, the successes and failures, the joys and sorrows of the people I am speaking to.

Third, God "redeems your life from the pit" (Psalm 103:4, ESV). What a great price it was!

> "You know the grace of our Lord Jesus Christ, that though he was rich, yet for your sake he became poor, so that you through his poverty might become rich" (2 Corinthians 8:9, NIV).

At Calvary, He not only redeemed our souls from damnation, but He also redeemed our lives from devastation, destruction and death.

Fourth, God "crowns you [lavishly] with lovingkindness and tender mercy" (Psalm 103:4, AMP). God now takes us into the throne room. He is going to crown us in grand style.

When God commanded the seas to swarm with fish, did He say, "Let the waters bring forth fish"? No! He used a superlative. He said: "Let the waters swarm and abundantly produce living creatures" (Genesis 1:20, AMP).

When Moses and Miriam and the children of Israel raised the first anthem song on the sands of Sinai after the Egyptian army had been swept away, how did Moses put it? "The LORD has triumphed"? No! He used a superlative; "The LORD has triumphed gloriously" (Exodus 15:1, AMP).

So here in Psalm 103 God is going to crown us. With what? "With kindness and mercy?" No! He is going to "crown us [lavishly] with lovingkindness and tender mercy" (Psalm 103:4, AMP).

Fifth, God "satisfies your years with good things, so that your youth is renewed like the [soaring] eagle" (Psalm 103:5, AMP). How wonderful it is that God does that.

Conclusion

Howard Hughes was the wealthiest man in the world in his day. He died at the age of seventy with fame and fortune, with all that the world has to offer. His estate was probated at approximately two and one half billion dollars. He was rarely seen in public for the last twenty years of his life. He spent his final years mostly in pajamas, living on fudge and cake. He suffered from malnutrition and weighed only ninety pounds when he died.

In contrast, David in his advancing age, raises this poem of praise to God:

"Bless the LORD, O my soul, and all that is within me,
Bless his holy name!
Bless the LORD, O my soul,
And forget not all his benefits" (Psalm 103:1-2, ESV).

So David concludes in the same way he commences. He returns to the beginning with this crowning comment: "Bless the LORD, O my soul!" (Psalm 103:22, ESV).

Such will be our praise in an endless eternity!

2.

A VISIT FROM JESUS ON THE JOURNEY

Abraham waited for twenty-five years for the birth of his son, Isaac. Nights of waiting. Have you been waiting for years for the birth of your first child?

Moses waited for forty years in the backside of the Midian desert waiting on sheep before he led the Israelites out of Egypt. Long nights of waiting. He was in the Egyptian palace for forty years as the Pharaoh-in waiting.

Elijah waited by the bubbling brook Cherith for three years. Have you ever experienced waiting for nights for that check to come in the mail? I have. Times without number.

Noah waited for one-hundred-and-twenty years before God sent rain. Have you ever wondered when God's "showers of blessing"[24] are going to come to you? I have. Imagine the nights of mockery and ridicule for Noah. People in general and your family in particular wonder but dare not ask out loud: "He responded to God's call, but God has not provided for him."

Even Jesus experienced rejection from his own family! "For not even His brothers believed in Him" (John 7:5, AMP), because they thought "He is out of His mind" (Mark 3:21, NKJV).

Paul waited on God for three years in the desert of Arabia. Nights in the seminary seem like an eternity. When will God put you to work? I've been there.

From the time that Joseph was thrown into the pit by his brothers to the time that he became Prime Minister in the Egyptian palace, Joseph had waited for thirteen years! Nights in the pit and yes, even in prison.

Acts 16

In Acts 16, Paul and Silas were brutally beaten, physically pummeled and thrown into a dungeon. They were beaten and bloodied, bruised and bound hand and foot in wooden stocks. The pain from the beating compounded by being forced into an unnatural and uncomfortable position. What did they do when they reached the depths of discouragement, disillusionment, and despair?

> "About midnight Paul and Silas were praying and singing hymns to God, and the prisoners were listening to them" (Acts 16:25, AMP).

This is what the songwriter has in mind when she writes:

> Some midnight hour, if you should find
> You're in a prison, in your mind
> Sing out in praise, defy the chains
> And they will fall in Jesus' name.[25]

If you listen intently to God, you will hear Him harmonizing with you at the "midnight hour" (Acts 16:25, KJV) of your life. Paul's Philippian prison became a place of praise. Like with the psalmist, you and I will rise to praise Him at midnight (Psalm 119:62). Remember that God is not going to replace your suffering with glory; rather He will transform your suffering into glory.[26]

God will meet you in the desperately difficult hours in the night because "Yours is the day, Yours also is the night" (Psalm 74:16, NASB). "Weeping may linger for the night, but joy comes in the morning" (Psalm 30:5, NRSV).

In the face of daily difficulties, remember the simple but straightforward words of Joseph:

> "God sent me ahead of you ... God sent me [to Egypt] ahead of you ... it was not you who sent me here, but God ..." (Genesis 45:5, 7-8, AMP).

What an amazing admission:

> "But God sent me ahead of you ... it was not you who sent me here but God" (Genesis 45:8, 9; cf. Genesis 50:20, NIV).

Joseph sees God as the central character in the recording chambers of his memory because he sees God's divine plans and purposes behind them all.

Writing of Joseph, F. B. Meyer, the English pastor, profoundly pens:

> "It is very sweet, as life passes by, to be able to look back on dark and mysterious events, and to trace the hand of God where we once saw only the malice and cruelty of man."[27]

"Fourth Watch of the Night"

You will find, as I have, that God specializes in operating in the night hours of our lives. Why? I'll tell you why. Because there are four watches in the night in the way the Hebrews count time, notice that the psalmist mentions the word "watches" five times. In other words, while we are asleep, God watches over us. We think of God while He watches over us: "I think of you through the watches of the night" (Psalm 63:6, NIV). That's a thrilling thought!

> "He who *watches* over you will not slumber ... indeed he who *watches* … will neither slumber nor sleep. The LORD *watches* over you ... The LORD will *watch* over your life; the LORD will *watch* over your coming and going both now and forevermore" (Psalm 121: 3-5; 7-8, NIV).

One thing is certain: God's plans for you are perfect, and they will all work out for your good and for His glory.

> "For I know the plans I have for you," declares the LORD, "plans to prosper you and not to harm you, plans to give you hope and a future" (Jeremiah 29:11, NIV).

Life may be full of difficulties and disappointments. Times may be tough, turbulent, and tumultuous, and people may be demanding and cause you to swallow your sorrows, but never forget that life is special.

Life is made up of moments. Trust God in the pain of the moments, even though the process may be long.

Frightening fears may buffet you with brutal blows. The prolific prophet in the Old Testament tells us why we have nothing to fear:

> "Do not fear, for I have redeemed you; I have called you by name; you are Mine. When you pass through the waters, I will be with you; And through the rivers, they will not overflow you. When you walk through the fire, you will not be scorched, nor will the flame burn you. For I am the LORD your God, The Holy One of Israel, your Savior; … Because you are precious in My sight, you are honored and I love you, … Do not fear, for I am with you" (Isaiah 43:1-5, AMP).

Listen to each reassurance from the prophet's pen. You have nothing to fear. Indeed, you have no one to fear.

> "And in the fourth watch of the night (3:00-6:00 a.m.), Jesus came to them (disciples) walking on the sea" (Matthew 14:25, AMP).

You will discover, as I have, that Jesus is never in a hurry. He is always right on time. He will come to you "in the fourth watch of the night." Because God watches over you and me, has it occurred to you that He is always with you when it is three o'clock in the morning?

The Methodist minister, William Poole, was a prolific hymnwriter. He records this profound truth in these memorable lyrics:

Just when I need Him, Jesus is near,
Just when I falter, just when I fear;
Ready to help me, ready to cheer,
Just when I need Him most.[28]

I pray that Jesus will meet you "in the fourth watch of the night," and that you will hear Him speaking to you: "Take courage, it is I! Do not be afraid" (Matthew 14:27, AMP). And may that same God come to you as He came to Solomon in the night and said:

"Ask [Me] what I shall give you" (1 Kings 3:5, AMP).

Say, what will your answer be?

3.

A HUMBLE HEART NEEDED FOR THE JOURNEY

A humble heart is a non-negotiable qualification for leadership. The humble person has the vision to see God's hand in another's life and applaud it. John Ruskin is right on target:

> "I believe that the first test of a truly great man is his humility. I do not mean by humility, doubt of one's one power. But really great men have a curious feeling that the greatness is not in them, but through them. And they see something divine in every other man and are endlessly, foolishly, incredibly merciful."[29]

John the Baptist was immensely influential. Yet the motto of his short life and ministry can be summarized in these seven words:

"He must increase, but I must decrease" (John 3:30, NKJV).

John called himself a lamp; but to him Jesus was the Light. John was only a man; Jesus was the Messiah.

What is Humility?

François Fénelon, an eighteenth-century Christian mystic, wrote that "all saints are convinced that sincere humility is the foundation of all virtues."[30] William Law, the great Anglican writer agrees:

> "[Humility] is so essential to the right state of our souls that there is no pretending to a reasonable or pious life without it. We may as well think to see without eyes or live without breath as to live in the spirit of religion without the spirit of humility."[31]

And what is humility? In part, Fénelon tells us, it is:

> "a certain honesty, and childlike willingness to acknowledge our faults, to recover from them, and to submit to the advice of experienced people; these will be solid useful virtues, adapted to your sanctification."[32]

Secret of Humility

This is the secret of humility: a constant commitment to the increase of Christ and the decrease of self. John had his own congregation and his own disciples. Yet John spoke of another whose leadership they should follow. Watch what happens:

> "Again the next day John was standing with two of his disciples, and he looked at Jesus as He walked, and said, 'Behold, the Lamb of God!' The two disciples heard him speak, and they followed Jesus" (John 1:35-37, NASB).

John's own disciples began applauding another leader. John recognizes that he is only the best man at the wedding, and Jesus is the bridegroom:

> "'I am not the Christ,' but, 'I have been sent ahead of Him.' He who has the bride is the bridegroom; but the friend of the bridegroom, who stands and hears him, rejoices greatly because of the bridegroom's voice. So this joy of mine has been made full" (John 3:28-29, NASB).

Our Responsibility

Like John, we have three responsibilities: to clear the way for the Lord, to prepare the way for the Lord, and to get out of the way of the Lord![33] To clear the way and prepare the way as John did is difficult, but the challenge is to get out of the way.

John knew that he could not simultaneously accept the glory and give God the glory. Jesus' glory is woven in his attitude and his actions. This timeless truth is a beautiful blend of courage and wisdom. Whether in his fame and fortune, public applause and appreciation, John's goal remains the same:

> "He must increase, but I must decrease" (John 3:30, NKJV).

John revealed more of his human frailty when, as a prisoner in Herod's dungeon and a prisoner of his own doubt and despair, he sent two of his disciples to Jesus with a question:

> "Are You the Expected One, (the Messiah), or should we look for someone else?" (Luke 7:19, AMP).

The most baffling times in my faith journey have been times when God acted in ways that were contrary to my expectations. Like us, John did not always understand God's ways. He stumbled. He abandoned hope. He lost confidence. He reached the depths of discouragement in a desert of delusion. But unlike us, John was willing to be transparent, honest, and vulnerable. What Charles Bridges writes is absolutely amazing:

> "On no point is the mind of God more fully declared than against pride … A lowly spirit ... is a most adorning grace. Nor is it an occasional or temporary feeling … but a habit, 'clothing' the man … 'from the sole of the foot to the head.' … He pours it [grace] out plentifully upon humble hearts."[34]

God will not bless what springs from pride. As the sword of Scripture repeatedly reminds us, He brings His mighty hand down over our lives and presses His sovereign fingers where it hurts. We sigh, we squirm, we struggle, and prayerfully, we submit (1 Peter 5:5-6).

Being committed to Christ's increase means acknowledging that He is supreme and that His image is more important than our own. It also means letting our lives function as a frame that shows up the masterpiece that is Jesus Christ.

Whether in days of delight or days of distress, John sought to exalt and elevate his God. This should be our conscious and constant thought. With calm and composure, Richard Bube reminds us:

> "Man cannot serve both self and God … The first step toward serving God … requires that we constantly and consciously put down the demands of self and surrender our desires to the Lord."[35]

Indeed, exalting the living Lord should be our greatest delight. Just as the sun's brightness eclipses the glow of the morning star, so Christ's glory should outshine our own.

May our theme in life be encapsulated in the lyrics of Andraé Crouch:

> To God be the glory
> For the things He has done.[36]

4.

PERSONAL DISCIPLINE NEEDED FOR THE JOURNEY

Personal discipline is the indispensable key for accomplishing anything in life.

The three-minute speech I delivered at QBC's 60th Anniversary on November 27th, 2022, was rewritten fifteen different times over the course of five months!

When it came to writing, Ernest Hemingway was the quintessence of discipline. His early writing was characterized by obsessive literary perfectionism as he labored to develop his economy of style, spending hours polishing a sentence, or searching for the right word. It is a well-known fact that he rewrote the conclusion to his novel *A Farewell to Arms*[37] seventeen times to get it right.

We wonder at the perfection of a da Vinci painting. But we forget that Leonardo da Vinci on one occasion drew a thousand hands.[38]

Churchill wrote everything out and practiced it! The margins of his manuscripts carried notes anticipating the "cheers," "hear, hears," "prolonged cheering," and even "standing ovation." This done, he practiced in front of mirrors, fashioning his retorts and facial expressions. Churchill's painstaking preparation freed him to give great impromptu speeches. F. E. Smith said, "Winston has spent the best years of his life writing impromptu speeches."[39]

Thomas Edison came up with the incandescent light after a thousand failures.

Discipline is everything!

The statement from Paul to Timothy regarding spiritual discipline takes on urgency:

> "Train yourself to be godly. Physical training is good, but training for godliness is much better, promising benefits in this life and in the life to come" (1 Timothy 4:7-8, NLT).

How? The writer of Hebrews explains it like this:

> "Therefore, since we are surrounded by such a great cloud of witnesses, let us throw off everything that hinders and the sin that so easily entangles. And let us run with perseverance the race marked out for us" (Hebrews 12:1, NIV).

We will never get anywhere spiritually without a conscious divestment of the things that are holding us back. What things are weighing you down?

Discipline demands that you throw it off. No discipline, no discipleship.

5.

GOD CALLS YOU BY NAME ON THE JOURNEY

It was "early Sunday morning while it was still dark" (John 20:1, NLT). Those are the exact words that John the beloved disciple wrote about that first Easter Sunday morning.

Mary Magdalene visited the tomb darkened by the shadows of silent Saturday. The only thing she expected to find was the cold, dead, lifeless, lonely body of Jesus.

Little did she know that dawn was breaking and hope was rising.

Someone met her at the tomb, and Mary thought that he was the gardener. This stranger asked Mary, "Why are you crying?"

Mary Magdalene, not knowing who was speaking to her, said: "Just give me Jesus!"

And the next thing she hears someone call her name, "Mary." In that moment, the gospel becomes not just powerful; it becomes personal.

When she hears her name, her eyes are opened, and she recognizes that He is not the gardener after all; this here is Christ Jesus.

And I am telling you this because Jesus is still calling your name.

> He knows my name,
> He knows my every thought.
> He sees each tear that falls
> And hears me when I call.[40]

Not only does Jesus know you by name, but He also calls you by name.

One by one He is calling our names; not just because the gospel is powerful, but because the gospel is personal.

He knows me. He knows you. He knows where we've been. He knows what we've done. He knows our weaknesses. He knows our strengths. He knows the places in our lives where we need His grace and mercy.

Like Mary, He does not discard us. He does not marginalize us. He comes to the disenfranchised, and the people like me who need a Savior, and He speaks our names.

And when our hearts warm with the conviction that only the Holy Spirit can bring, we respond just like Mary. Our eyes are opened because we realize that He is who He says He is, and He is still able to accomplish what He says:

> "'I know the plans I have for you,' declares the Lord, 'plans to prosper you, and not to harm you: plans to give you a hope and a future'" (Jeremiah 29:11, NIV).

Our eyes are opened. Was it Paul who said:

> "No eye has seen, no ear has heard, and no mind has imagined what God has prepared for those who love Him"? (1 Corinthians 2:9, NLT).

Mary races away becoming the first Evangelist telling everyone what her eyes have seen and what her ears have heard.

So on early Easter Sunday morning, we can sing:

> Because He lives, I can face tomorrow.
> Because He lives, all fear is gone.
> Because I know He holds the future,
> And life is worth the living,
> Just because He lives![41]

6.

GOD ONLY CALLS SINFUL PEOPLE FOR THE JOURNEY

God only calls sinful people. That's us.

Do you remember Elijah slumped into a deep depression? Do you remember he fled into the woods, hid under a juniper tree and prayed for the Lord to take his life? The story recorded in 1 Kings 19 is worth a second look.

Not only did Elijah run because he was intimidated by Jezebel, but he also ran because he really believed that there was no one else quite as dedicated as he. Listen to Elijah as he pouted:

> "I have been very zealous for the LORD, the God of hosts; for the sons of Israel have forsaken Your covenant, torn down Your altars and killed Your prophets with the sword. And I alone am left; and they seek my life, to take it away" (1 Kings 19:14, NASB).

Without a hint of hesitation, God interrupted his pity-party and informed him that there were seven thousand others, like Elijah, who had not bowed to Baal.

When God calls people to serve Him, He calls only sinful people. Not even one could claim perfection. Each one is inadequate, weak, and wayward by nature. We could pose for a portrait painted in the words by Robert Robinson:

> Prone to wander, Lord, I feel it;
> Prone to leave the God I love.[42]

Stroll slowly with me through sacred Scriptures. A brief review of biblical characters will help. Peter denied Jesus three times ever so deliberately and decisively in the dark only hours after promising to be true to Christ. John Mark deserted Paul and Barnabas on their first missionary journey when they needed him the most. Demas "having loved this present world," forsook Paul and fled to Thessalonica (2 Timothy 4:10, NASB).

What about the prodigal prophet Jonah? God used him to lead a spiritual awakening in Nineveh. An entire city repented. Jonah wanted destruction, but God gave deliverance. Gehazi, Elisha's servant, could not hide his greed.

David became "a man after [God's] own heart" (Acts 13:22, NASB), yet his life was soiled by a sordid sex scandal (see 2 Samuel 11). Aaron prompted the molding of a golden calf for the Hebrews to worship. Samson was a womanizer.

No one is immune to imperfection. None of the above and neither you nor me. If it can happen to them, it can happen to us.

That's why I am grateful for Jesus who says, "… but I have prayed for you, that your faith may not fail …" (Luke 22:32, NASB).

Christ Jesus is the only One who is pristine, pure, and perfect. He is the only One who can guarantee you a home in heaven. He is the only One who can forgive your sins. He is the only One who can see "the very thoughts and intentions of the heart" (Hebrews 4:12, AMP). He is the only One whose death paid the debt for your sins.

It has been my privilege to serve Him for over fifty years.

This morning I woke up with this hymn on my lips. This is my prayer and commitment. May it be yours also.

> May I be willing, Lord, to bear
> Daily my cross for Thee;
> Even Thy cup of grief to share,
> Thou hast borne all for me.
>
> Fill me, O Lord, with Thy desire
> For all that know not Thee;
> Then touch my lips with holy fire,
> To speak of Calvary.[43]

7.

GOD OF ALL YOUR MOMENTS ON THE JOURNEY

Wouldn't you love the ability to go back in time and change something you did or said? I know there have been moments in my life when I acted on the impulse of the flesh that I would dearly love to call back.

During the days prior to his homegoing, Moses would have gladly given his right arm to relive that incident at the rock. But he could not go back.

In a single moment of rage, he forfeited his right to lead Israel and threw away the opportunity to enter the Promised Land. As I ponder that tiny slice of time in Moses' life, my mind ranges through the Scriptures to a few such moments:

- What would Eve give for another chance before the tree in the Garden of Eden?
- What would David give to relive that night on the rooftop when he first saw Bathsheba?

We cannot go back. None of us can. We cannot undo sinful deeds or unsay sinful words.

Like Moses, we may be forgiven for those sins and have them blotted out of our record by the blood of Christ. Even so, we must live with the consequences of our words and our actions. The word of warning from Scriptures is:

> "Do not be deceived, God is not mocked [He will not allow Himself to be ridiculed, nor treated with contempt nor allow His precepts to be scornfully set aside]; for whatever a man sows, this and this only is what he will reap" (Galatians 6:7, AMP).

I do not want my testimony for Jesus Christ to be shattered by a single moment of indulging my flesh. I do not want one moment of rage or pride or arrogance to cast a shadow over a lifetime of walking with my Lord. I fear that possibility. I want to fear that possibility. When I stop fearing it, I am in dire danger.

David once prayed this great prayer. Will you allow me to pray this verse over you? The Living Bible renders it in this way:

> "Keep your servant from deliberate sins! Don't let them control me. Then I will be free of guilt and innocent of great sin" (Psalm 19:13).

Our gracious God has covered our past with His own blood, given on the cross for us. David reminds us that:

> "As far as the east is from the west, so far has He removed our transgressions from us" (Psalm 103:12, NASB).

You can learn to walk closely with your God day by day, hour by hour, and moment by moment because He is the God of all your moments.

I close with the reassuring lyrics from that old hymn, "Day by Day":

> Day by day and with each passing moment,
> Strength I find to meet my trials here;
> Trusting in my Father's wise bestowment,
> I've no cause for worry or for fear.
>
> He whose heart is kind beyond all measure
> Gives unto each day what he deems best –
> Lovingly, its part of pain and pleasure,
> Mingling toil with peace and rest.[44]

8.
OUR CALLING ON THE JOURNEY

Ray Stedman, the late prominent pastor of Peninsula Bible Church in Palo Alto, California, utters these unforgettable words:

> "It's not our relationship with Jesus Christ which counts before the world, it is our resemblance to him."[45]

God calls us to live out our faith in the midst of a pagan and post-Christian culture. We are deluged daily by the clamor of our culture. D. A. Carson observes:

> "The church of Jesus Christ has conformed so thoroughly to this environment that it is often difficult to see how it differs in these matters from contemporary paganism."[46]

One cultural observer warns that America is on the brink of collapse. He writes:

> "America presents unsettling parallels with the disintegration of Rome – a decline of moral values, a loss of political civility, an overextended military, an inability to control national borders, and the growth of fiscal irresponsibility by the central government. Does this sound familiar?"[47]

The Beatitudes are simple sounding, but they are a radical rearrangement of our value systems, daring us to be different. In the Beatitudes, Jesus speaks in the third person: "Blessed are those," and "blessed are they." When He talks about shaking salt[48] and shining light, He subtly shifts the pronouns from the third person to the second person: "You are the salt of the earth. You are the light of the world ..." (Matthew 5:13-14).

These are incredible statements. Simple but profound. And don't miss that emphatic "you" in both those statements: "You are the salt of the earth. You are the light of the world."

What Bishop N. T. Wright writes is helpful:

> "And God, who sees and loves all alike, wants the church to reflect [his] generous, universal love in how it behaves."[49]

Not the flamboyant few. Not those who have been to seminary. Not those who have been ordained. But all who know Christ Jesus as Savior. Everyone in God's forever family is to be shaking salt and shining light.

Salt defeats decay. Light dispels darkness. Too much salt ruins the food just as too much light blinds the eyes.

Stumbling Saints

Christians are not the first to limp along in our calling to live as salt and light. Throughout human history, there are many biblical examples of stumbling saints: Noah's drunkenness, Abraham's misogyny, Jacob's lies, Jesse's parental neglect, David's adultery and murder, Solomon's womanizing, Elijah's self-pity, Peter's cowardice, to name a few.

Today we live in a time of moral and spiritual crisis every bit as dire and dangerous as the saints who have gone before us. In his excellent exposition of Jesus' Sermon on the Mount, Pastor Martyn Lloyd-Jones said that Christians become a light to the world to the degree that they stand out as different from the world. He writes:

> "The glory of the gospel is that when the church is absolutely different from the world, she invariably attracts it."[50]

The novelist and poet Madeleine L'Engle writes that:

> "We draw people to Christ not by loudly discrediting what they believe, by telling them how wrong they are and how right we are, but by showing them a light that is so lovely that they want with all their hearts to know the source of it."[51]

Pastor John R. W. Stott injects humor in what he says:

> "I sometimes think how splendid it would be if non-Christians, curious to discover the secret and source of our light, were to come up to us and enquire:
>
> Twinkle, twinkle, little star,
> How I wonder what you are!"[52]

And then you get to light their way home!

Shine your light into the darkness; that's where it is really needed. "Darkness can be driven away only by light."[53]

C. T. Studd was an English missionary who served God in China, India, and Africa. I appreciate his wonderful and welcome reminder:

> "Some wish to live within the sound
> Of Church or Chapel bell;
> I want to run a Rescue Shop
> Within a yard of hell."[54]

The horrific behavior of some Christians, whether historic or contemporary, can serve to delegitimize the entire Christian movement. This is why Mahatma Gandhi says:

> "I like your Christ, but I do not like your Christians. Your Christians are so unlike your Christ."[55]

A San Francisco journalist, Herb Caen says,

> "The trouble with born-again Christians is that they are an even bigger pain the second time around."[56]

Marion Jacobsen expresses my convictions perfectly:

> "People are hungry for acceptance, love and friends, and unless they find them in the church, they may not stay there long enough to become personally related to Jesus Christ … People are not persuaded – they are attracted. We must be able to communicate far more by what we are than by what we say."[57]

At eighty-one, Evangeline Booth, then general of the Salvation Army, was asked when she had first wanted to be a part of the Salvation Army. She answers:

"Very early. I saw my parents (founders of the Salvation Army) working for their people, bearing their burdens. Day and night. They did not have to say a word to me about Christianity."[58]

Consider Christ

Is the poor behavior of some Christians sufficient reason to excuse ourselves from considering Christ Himself? Are the many failures, as offensive as they may be, enough to override and overrule an empty tomb? Will we lose respect for Mozart if a drunk person plays his music poorly at a dinner party?

As important as it is to represent Jesus well to a watching world, Christians' failure to do so is no good reason to dismiss the "Man Christ Jesus, who gave Himself as a ransom [a substitutionary sacrifice to atone] for all …" (1 Timothy 2:5-6, AMP).

It is only through the sacrifice of our sinless Savior that we are made righteous. God made Jesus "who had no sin to be sin for us, so that in him we might become the righteousness of God" (2 Corinthians 5:21, NIV). Christ is the only One God honors because:

> Without the way, there is no going;
> Without the truth, there is no knowing;
> Without the life, there is no living.[59]

We are to make every effort to connect with and commit to the Person who is trustworthy and true. The hymnwriter puts it,

> That Christ has regarded [our] helpless estate
> And hath shed his own blood for [our] soul.[60]

The Sri Lankan evangelist, Daniel T. Niles said that participating in Christ's mission is like one beggar telling another beggar where to find food.[61]

Do those who are closest to us know that we are angry about the most insignificant things? That we have road rage. That we think more about money than we should. That we find more satisfaction in the praise of men than the glory of God. That we are afraid about the future as much as we trust God for it. That we live by fear as much as we live by faith.

Day after day. Week after week. Month after month. Spring, summer, fall, and winter. We are all being observed!

> "You are writing a gospel, a chapter each day,
> By deeds that you do, by words that you say.
> Men read what you write, whether faithless or true.
> Say, what is the gospel according to you?"[62]

Jesus repeatedly reminds us that "it is not praise that He desires; it is practice"[63] He delights in. His magnificent message on the Mount "is not to be commended, it is to be carried out."[64] I wholeheartedly agree with Wiersbe who writes:

> "We Christians boast that we are not ashamed of the gospel of Christ, but perhaps the gospel of Christ is ashamed of us. For some reason, our ministry doesn't match our message."[65]

When I see Jesus on the cross crying out, "My God, my God, why have you forsaken me?" (Matthew 27:46, NIV). I often think, "My God, why haven't you forsaken me?" The words of Brennan Manning ring true:

> "I am a bundle of paradoxes. I believe and I doubt, I hope and get discouraged, I love and I hate, I feel bad about feeling good, I feel guilty about not feeling guilty. I am trusting and suspicious. I am honest and I still play games."[66]

We must not try to pull ourselves up by our bootstraps. Rather, we must realize that we don't even have boots. We must not merely think that we have problems. Rather, we must understand that we are our own biggest problem. William Shakespeare's Cassius correctly concludes, "The fault, dear Brutus, is not in our stars but in ourselves."[67]

We are not alone in our frustrations and failures. The sins and setbacks that beset us play a key role in the way God intends to mold us in the person of His Son. It is from this posture that we recognize the truth that apart from Christ Jesus, we can do nothing (John 15:5).

Our Privilege

Because of Jesus' vicarious death on our behalf, we are to serve as the spokespersons for the pure and perfect One who is full of grace and truth and whose name is Holy. The privilege God has given us is the same privilege God gave to adulterous David, the murderous Paul, and the abrasive Peter.

Jesus invites us to come as we are. He does not want us to stay as we are. Jesus, our faithful Savior, will never leave us nor forsake us (Hebrews 13:5). And no earthly catastrophe can ever separate us from the grip of God's love (Romans 8:38-39).

No matter how deep our regrets or how checkered our past, there will never cease to be a place of belonging for us in our Father's house. We are to God as the disabled Mephibosheth was to king David – who for Jonathan's sake would never cease to have a seat at his king's table (2 Samuel 9:13). For Jesus' sake, we likewise will never cease to have a seat at our King's table.

9.

CHOOSING TO SERVE GOD ON THE JOURNEY

Etched in the annals of inspired Hebrew history, is recorded Joshua's final farewell. Prior to his death, Joshua, Moses' successor, stood before the elders of Israel and gave a soul-stirring speech:

> "If it is unacceptable in your sight to serve the LORD, choose for yourselves this day whom you will serve: whether the gods which your fathers served that were on the other side of the River, or the gods of the Amorites in whose land you live; but as for me and my house, we will serve the LORD" (Joshua 24:15, AMP).

Life is full of competing choices. When I decided to serve God in full time ministry in 1971, there were other choices I had to make like choosing a spouse, choosing a theological school, choosing a degree program, choosing where to live. These choices are life-changing.

I did not waver. Not a split-second of hesitation.

I carefully considered and confidently chose.

I turned my eyes away from everything and fully focused and firmly fixed my eyes on Christ. Until your eyes are fixed on the Lord, you will not be able to endure days that go from bad to worse. That's how I know I made the correct choice.

In *The Healing Power of Stories*, Daniel Taylor comments that "both the present and the future are determined by choices."[68]

When Christ invades your life, He inhabits your future. From the rising of the sun to the setting of the same, God's personal promise to you is recorded in Jeremiah's journal:

> "For I know the plans I have for you … plans to prosper you and not to harm you, plans to give you hope and a future" (Jeremiah 29:11, NIV).

What do people want today? They want a model. They want a model that's authentic. But modeling must accompany our message.

People respond better to personal models than to verbal demands. That's why Joshua said: "But as for me and my house, we will serve the LORD" (Joshua 24:15, ESV).

So it was in Joshua's day. The leader had made up his mind. He and his household would serve the Lord. But when it came to everyone else, "choose for yourselves today whom you will serve" (Joshua 24:15, NASB).

Drawn by Joshua's commitment, the Hebrews chose to align themselves with his cause. Joshua's desires became their desires. Joshua's dedication became their dedication. If you delve deeply into this section of Scripture, you will see their threefold decision.

Firstly, they chose to "fear the LORD" (Joshua 24:14, AMP).

Secondly, they chose to "serve Him in sincerity" (Joshua 24:14, NASB). Notice on three separate and subsequent occasions, they declared their courageous commitment "to serve the LORD" (Joshua 24:18, 21, 24, NASB).

Thirdly, they chose to "obey His voice" (Joshua 24:24, NASB). They announced their decision to obey the Lord.

It is not coincidental that the first verse I learned in Sunday School was:

> "Behold, to obey is better than sacrifice,
> And to hearken than the fat of rams" (1 Samuel 15:22, KJV).

It is not only valid, but in fact, vital from ample Scriptural support, that God honors you when you choose to obey Him. He takes you at your word, and He weaves His power into the fabric of your lives. He supplements your desires with His ability.

What Theodore Epp has written is apt and apropos: "Once a man is satisfied that he is in the center of God's plan and God is working out His will through him, that man is invincible."[69]

If you make the right choice, it will stand the test of time. For me, it has been more than fifty years.

10.

RESPONDING TO GOD'S CALL FOR THE MINISTRY JOURNEY

Did you hear God's voice? Have you forgotten that voice? That voice comes from God's heart, and it is calling your name. Like the bush that keeps burning, God's voice keeps calling. With exquisite eloquence, Pastor F. B. Meyer writes:

> "... A common bush began to shine with the emblem of Deity; and from its heart of fire the voice of God broke the silence of the ages in words that fell on the shepherd's ear like a double-knock: 'Moses, Moses.' And from that moment all his life was altered."[70]

Moses' journey of obedience commenced when he knelt on the silent summit of Sinai, and concluded when he stood on the steep slopes of Pisgah, overlooking the Promised Land.

I look longingly back to that day which came unannounced and unheralded. One greater than Moses spoke to me in sunny Singapore in September 1971 from His wonderful Word:

> "If anyone serves me, he must follow me; and where I am, there shall my servant be also; if anyone serves me, the Father will honor him" (John 12:26, RSV).

God first appeared to me at the crackling campfire in Port Dickson, Malaysia. For nine months, I had resisted God's call on my life. For nine months, I had said, "No." In retrospect, I wish that my resistance to God out of sheer stubbornness did not last so long. A competent commentator of yesteryear said it succinctly: "They who disobey do not believe; and they who do not believe disobey."[71]

Moses' Argument

With incisive insight, C. S. Lewis writes: "To argue with God is to argue with the very power that makes it possible to argue at all."[72]

Woven into the fabric of Exodus 3 and 4 is a dialogue. It's really an argument. That specific section of Scripture records this scene. God is saying "Go" and Moses is answering "No."

God initiates the invitation in the shadow of Sinai: "… come now, and I will send you to Pharaoh, so that you may bring My people, the sons of Israel, out of Egypt" (Exodus 3:10, NASB).

Has Moses heard that voice before? Yes. But that was four decades ago. That was forty long years ago. For me, it has been fifty-two years since I heard His call!

Listen to Moses' argument. "Who am I?" (Exodus 3:11). Was Moses' voice dripping with defiance?

God uses nobodies. He makes nobodies into somebodies. The fact is He does remarkable things through nobodies.

The eminent evangelist of yesteryear, D. L. Moody describes Moses in these memorable words:

> "Moses spent his first forty years thinking he was a somebody. He spent his second forty years learning he was a nobody. He spent his third forty years discovering what God can do with a nobody."[73]

You and I live in one of those three stages. We either think we are somebody, or we realize that we are nobody, or we have discovered what God can do with a nobody!

God's Answer

"Who am I?" (Exodus 3:11). I love God's answer! From the mouth of the living Lord comes words that are laced with encouragement: "Certainly I will be with you … when you have brought the people out of Egypt" (Exodus 3:12, NASB). Notice God said when, not if.

When you and I look back on our own lives, we will say, "We really cannot explain how, but God did it."

Moses was still reticent. Indeed, he was hesitant. Moses' argument continues into Exodus 4. Here he carps and complains. He passionately poured out his heart as he unleashes multiple missiles from his arsenal of fear.

> "Please, Lord, I have never been eloquent, neither recently nor in time past, nor since Thou hast spoken to Thy servant, for I am slow of speech and slow of tongue" (Exodus 4:10, NASB).

Moses' first forty years was nothing short of impressive. His résumé was remarkable. He was capable and confident as a speaker. The sacred Scriptures declare that Moses "was a man of power in words and deeds" (Acts 7:22, AMP). But the stinging sands of the Midian Desert robbed him of the confidence he once had.

God's Accomplishments

God commands, "Go, and I'll be with your mouth" (Exodus 4:12, NASB). That's breathtakingly beautiful! Time and again, through over fifty years of preaching, He "has been with my mouth."

God talks to Moses in the fire. As with Moses, the fire of God burned out all my excuses. As with Moses, God touched my mouth, and allowed me to speak of His grace not only in Singapore, in Malaysia, in Indonesia, in Israel, but also in over one thousand churches across the United States of America.

Fanny J. Crosby has written over 8,000 hymns over the course of her ninety-five years. What's even more remarkable is that she was blind since she was six months old. What Crosby wonderfully wrote has been my lifelong prayer:

Consecrate me now to Thy service, Lord,
By the pow'r of grace divine;
Let my soul look up with a steadfast hope,
And my will be lost in Thine.[74]

What's Your Excuse?

You say, "Pastor, I can't speak with ease and efficiency." "I do not have strong family support." "I do not have adequate financial resources." My dear brother and sister, your clever and creative excuses will not stand a chance either.

As with Moses and others, God will be with your mouth. Many, if not most, of you have supportive families who encourage you and pray for you.

Queenstown Baptist Church supported me for the first two years (1975-1976) I was a student at Singapore Bible College to the tune of $85 a month. When the support ceased, I gave private tuition to three primary school-aged students to subsidize my limited income.

I had four jobs from 1975-1978. I was a full-time student at SBC. I was a pastor at Jurong Baptist Church. I preached weekly, led Wednesday night Bible Studies and prayer meetings, visited Jurong neighborhood high-rises on Saturdays; I gave private tuition three nights a week, and I was dating Rose. Needless to say, I did not have much time for mischief.

Rose and I left Singapore for San Francisco on December 18th, 1978, with $1,000 in our pockets, not knowing one single person in America. Not one single individual or one single church in Singapore entered into partnership with us. In the face of these seemingly insurmountable and inconceivable odds, there was "no one but God"[75] whom we could count on. Indeed, "the One who feeds the sparrow, Is the One who stands by [us.]"[76] The God "who calls you is faithful," and He delights to surprise you by exceeding your expectations (1 Thessalonians 5:24, NASB).

Are you still wrestling with God's call on your life right now? How long will you resist God before you say "Yes" to Him?

Are you still arguing with God? It's fruitless to argue with Him. I argued with God for nine months in 1971. He won. And I have been serving Him in full time ministry since 1975.

Love God wholeheartedly. Love God willingly. Hold nothing back, because in the words of C. T. Studd, the missionary who served God in China, India, and Africa:

> "One life 'twill soon be past,
> Only what's done for Christ will last."[77]

One of my favorite poets is Amy Carmichael. This is what she writes:

> "Give me the love that leads the way,
> The faith that nothing can dismay,
> The hope no disappointments tire,
> The passion that will burn like fire,
> Let me not sink to be a clod:
> Make me Thy fuel, flame of God."[78]

God is looking for someone like you with ears to hear His voice, hands ready to do His work, and a heart that is willing to respond.

How long will it take for you to respond to Him?

My prayer and plea is that you will not only say, but sing:

> I have decided to follow Jesus,
> I have decided to follow Jesus,
> I have decided to follow Jesus,
> No turning back, no turning back.
>
> Though none go with me, I still will follow,
> Though none go with me, I still will follow,
> Though none go with me, I still will follow,
> No turning back, no turning back[79]

A professor of history once said: "If Columbus had turned back, no one would have blamed him but nobody would have remembered him either."[80] I pray that you will not turn back from following our Lord.

You are at the crucial crossroads of your life. You are about to make one of the most important decisions as a Christ-follower. May God grant you His grace as you discern and determine to invest your life for eternity.

11.

CLOSED DOORS ON THE JOURNEY

Do you only thank God when He opens doors for you?

In Acts 16:6-9, Paul wanted to go to Phrygia, God says, "No." He wanted to go to Galatia, God says "No." He wanted to go to Mysia, God says "No." He wanted to go to Bithynia, God says "No." Four doors slammed shut in Paul's face.

What makes Acts 16 so special and significant is that it comes after Paul experienced four closed doors. The God who closed four doors is the same God who opened the door to Philippi.

May I turn your eyes and ears to our sovereign Savior "who opens, and no one will [be able to] shut, and ... who shuts, and no one opens" (Revelation 3:7, AMP). In the next verse, Christ declares: "I have put in front of you an open door that no one can shut" (Revelation 3:8, NET).

What would you do if you encountered the Executive Director of the Kentucky Baptist Convention in 1981 who tells you that you will never pastor an American church in Kentucky?

Who opens doors for you? Who opens doors for me? Listen to the words of our living and loving, Lord Jesus as He speaks life into your spiritual journey.

Not only did God open the door for us to serve Him in an American church in Spencer, Indiana, but He also opened doors to 250 churches in Indiana, Illinois, Ohio, Wisconsin, Michigan, and West Virginia in 5 years! 250 churches in 6 states in 5 years! (1982-1987).

I know "I Serve a Risen Savior"[81] because He opens doors for me as recently as this morning.

Had I listened to that "hotshot" in Kentucky, I would have missed 250 "open doors."

Whose voice are you listening to? The voice of man or the voice of God?

What God says to Paul, He says to you and me today:

> “A huge door of opportunity for effective work has opened up to me, and there are many adversaries” (1 Corinthians 16:9, AMP and MSG).

Oh, do you not know?

> “No eye has seen, no ear has heard, and no mind has imagined what God has prepared for those who love him” (1 Corinthians 2:9, NLT).

Start thanking Him for closing doors that will lead to the “huge door of opportunity for good work” (1 Corinthians 16:9, MSG).

12.

OPEN DOORS ON THE JOURNEY

Open Doors. Who opens doors for you? Who opens doors for me? Listen to the wonderful words of our living and loving Lord:

> "Behold, I have set before you an open door, which no one is able to shut" (Revelation 3:8, RSV).

The words, "have set" is in the perfect tense. Amazingly, I have discovered that when God speaks, He frequently uses the perfect tense.

For example, "Every place that the sole of your foot will tread upon I have given to you, as I promised to Moses" (Joshua 1:3, RSV). When God speaks here to Joshua, the first battle of Jericho has not been waged yet (Joshua 6), no victory has been experienced yet.

When the perfect tense is used in the Old and New Testaments, we call it the prophetic perfect. What does this mean? This means that when God speaks, it is as good as done.

So, when Christ says to you, "I have set before you an open door, which no one is able to shut," I want you to listen to Him with the ears of your heart. And when He says, "no one is able to shut," He means "no one." No human person. No demon. No deacon. Literally, no one is able to thwart the purposes of God in your life.

You are living in the days of unlimited opportunities, but you are also living in the days of unprecedented opposition. I am reminded that the venerable Paul says:

> "For a wide door for effective work has opened to me, and there are many adversaries" (1 Corinthians 16:9, RSV).

I have had the unique privilege of walking with and serving Christ for over fifty years, and I can bear witness to the fact that He who began a good work in you, will bring it to completion in you. What Jesus commences; Christ will complete. The Living Bible renders Philippians 1:6 in this way:

> "And I am sure that God who began the good work within you will keep right on helping you grow in his grace until his task within you is finally finished on that day when Jesus Christ returns."

Brothers and sisters do not wonder and fear if God is going to come through for you. God's purposes and plans for you will not be foiled or frustrated.

So, what is your response to Christ's open door? Get up and walk right through "the open door." His words are as current as this morning's news:

> "These are the words of him who is holy and true … What he opens no one can shut, and what he shuts no one can open" (Revelation 3:7, NIV).

God's blessings always lie on the other side of obedience. They multiply with the slow and silent passing of time.

13.

WAITING ON THE JOURNEY

Author and pastor Ben Patterson writes:

> "To wait on God is to trust your life to God in that way. The big difference is that the step of trust is a lifetime in the taking. It is a daily choice."[82]

Do you know of one person who loves to wait?

Abraham waited for twenty-five years for the birth of his son, Isaac. Moses waited for forty years in the backside of the Midian desert before he led the Israelites out of Egypt. Elijah waited by the bubbling brook Cherith. Noah waited for one-hundred-and-twenty years before God sent rain. Paul waited on God for three years in the desert of Arabia. From the time that Joseph was thrown into the pit by his brothers to the time that he became Prime Minister in the Egyptian palace, Joseph had waited for thirteen years!

In ministry, Rose and I have found that waiting is neither exciting nor eventful, especially if you are the one waiting. For us, waiting often seems like an eternity.

When you are in God's "waiting room," He is shaping you for a strategic and significant future. While you and I are waiting on God, oftentimes we cannot see that He is working behind the scenes.

God's delays are not God's denials. Our disappointments are God's appointments. V. Raymond Edman, for many decades the president of Wheaton College, expresses:

> "Delay … can be a deep discipline to the soul that would serve the Lord Jesus … The discipline of delay is written large in the life of God's people, as we could observe in Abraham's long waiting for the son of promise."[83]

God sometimes delays His answers. This is not because He lacks the power to answer our prayers. Nor is it because He lacks the desire to answer our prayers. God is not cruel, and He is not insensitive to our suffering. He delights in giving good gifts to His children.

"From Dan to Beersheba" is a biblical phrase that refers to Dan in the North and Beersheba in the South, a distance of more than twenty-seven-hundred miles. Whenever the Bible mentions that a saint goes in a southerly direction, it simply means that that person is running away from God.

Like with aging Abraham and Sarah, God will see us through the barrenness of Beersheba. Three men visited with Abraham and Sarah and announced: "At the appointed time I will return to you, at this time next year, Sarah will have a son" (Genesis 18:14, NASB).

Sure enough, Abraham was one hundred and Sarah was ninety when Isaac was born. Their sarcastic snickering turned into a laughter of pleasure and praise. Isaac means "He laughs."

Abraham and Sarah waited for twenty-five years for Isaac to be born!

God will meet you in your desperately difficult days at Beersheba and produce an Isaac in your life: "Is anything too hard for the LORD?" (Genesis 18:14, NLT). Or consider the questions from the preeminent prophet:

> "Who else has held the oceans in his hand? Who has measured off the heavens with his fingers? Who else knows the weight of the earth or has weighed the mountains and hills on a scale? Who is able to advise the Spirit of the LORD? Who knows enough to give him advice or teach him? Has the LORD ever needed anyone's advice? Does he need instruction about what is good? Did someone teach him what is right or show him the path of justice?" (Isaiah 40:12-14, NLT).

While we wait, God works. James Stalker writes no finer words than these:

> "Waiting is a common instrument of providential discipline for those to whom exceptional work has been appointed."[84]

14.

MONEY FOR THE MINISTRY JOURNEY

Money and ministry flow together. Few things are accomplished in ministry without money from God's special servants. Warren Wiersbe is right on target:

> "Ministry takes place when divine resources meet human needs through loving channels to the glory of God."[85]

Penetrating principles of the timeless truth of God's faithfulness are sprinkled throughout my recently published book, *Faith Journey.*[86] In this chapter, I shall attempt to provide a short, succinct summary of this sensitive subject which has caused many to question whether God has called them into full time ministry.

If God has provided for Rose and me in almost fifty years, He will provide for you. If God has opened doors to over one thousand churches in Anglo, Black, Hispanic, and Asian communities for us across the United States of America, surely, He can do the same for you. The question is: Do you trust Him to do it for you?

Promise and Provision

The Lord delights to surprise you with His goodness, if only you would unlock the door of obedience with the key of faith. Fervency and faith are intimately intertwined.

> "And at the seventh time the servant said, 'A cloud as small as a man's hand is coming up from the sea'" (1 Kings 18:43, AMP).

Elijah's eyes saw only a little charcoal cloud, but his eyes of faith saw the powerful promise of God.

The devotional commentator, Matthew Henry, is absolutely accurate:

> "The opening of our eyes will be the silencing of our fears. In the dark we are most apt to be frightened. The clearer sight we have of … the power of heaven, the less we shall fear the calamities of earth."[87]

The vision God gave me cleared away my confusion and brought me clarity – and it can do the same for you.

The promise of God always precedes the provision of God. These two timeless thoughts are closely connected. I have complete confidence in the promises of my Savior.

Was it not Jesus who reminded us that He will provide for our food and clothing? "Look at the birds of the air … and consider the lilies of the field," He implored (Matthew 6:26, 28 RSV).

Jean Caudill

In our last pastorate, God used a sister to bless me so that I could finish my doctoral work at Fuller Seminary.

Three weeks after we arrived at our new ministry assignment in Southern California, Jim and Jean Caudill invited us to their home on a Sunday afternoon. This is what Jean Caudill said to us: "When I invest in you, I'm investing in God's work!"[88] What encouraging words!

Nine months later, Jean received word that I had completed all the requirements for my doctoral work.

"Patrick, you need a doctoral robe. Here's why. There will be times in your ministry such as a baby dedication, a wedding, a funeral, or a graduation exercise when you will need to wear a robe."

This was my response. "Jean, that's such a waste of money." Before I could say another word, Jean gave me a check for the robe. "Now, go to the school tailor and get measured. All I ask is that you wear the robe one time on the Sunday after your graduation."

And I did. And she beamed from ear to ear.

A few years later, Jean Caudill went to be with the Lord. Parishioners were curious why I wore my doctoral robe. When I stood to the podium for the memorial service, this was what I said:

> "Not too long ago, someone told me that when I go to a graduation exercise, I might need to wear a robe. Ladies and gentlemen, today, I am going to Jean Caudill's graduation service in heaven, that's why I am wearing this robe that she gave me as a gift."

I could hardly finish my message that day.

"I Know Who Holds Tomorrow"

One of my favorite hymn writers is Ira Stanphill. In "I Know Who Holds Tomorrow," Stanphill writes these utterly unforgettable words from the depths of his own personal pain and loss:

> But the One who feeds the sparrow,
> Is the One who stands by me.[89]

The Precious People of Philippi

The Lord delights to surprise you by exceeding your expectations. From Paul's pen flows these wonderful words:

> "Nevertheless, you have done well to share with me in my difficulty. You yourselves also know, Philippians, that at the first preaching of the gospel, after I left Macedonia, no church shared with me in the matter of giving and receiving except you alone" (Philippians 4:14-15, NASB).

In his missionary journeys, Paul had numerous needs. He endured hardship, heartaches, and headaches. The Philippian partners felt pain when he hurt. They prayed for him when he was unable to stay in touch. They sent friends to comfort him when he was in prison. What a church! No wonder he felt such affection for them.

The precious people of Philippi were magnificent models in giving. "Even in Thessalonica" (Philippians 4:16). Even when Paul was in Thessalonica, the Philippian saints kept right on giving.

Now you know why Philippians is my favorite book in the New Testament.

Acts 16

The church at Philippi can best be appreciated when you read it in the context of Luke's letter. I am convinced that God is ready to send a Lydia into your life if you will trust Him (Acts 16:11-15, 40). Do not gloss over verse 40 in Acts 16. Why did Paul and Silas visit Lydia's home after they were released from prison, while they were still bruised and bleeding from the beating? I believe it's because there in Lydia's home, they knew they would find affirmation and affection, comfort and compassion. The rare and reassuring presence of these few faithful friends was invaluable. They loved Paul and Silas genuinely and they knew how to listen. Charles Bridges reminds us:

> "We gather knowledge when we listen; we spend it when we teach, but if we spend before we gather, we'll soon be bankrupt."[90]

Sophie Tucker was a Russian-born American singer, actress and comedienne. Her words are worthy of consideration:

> "From birth to eighteen, a girl needs good parents.
> From eighteen to thirty-five, she needs good looks.
> From thirty-five to fifty-five, she needs a good personality.
> From fifty-five on, she needs cash."[91]

Did I need cash when I responded to God's call to ministry? The Greek word is: "Yes!"

Miracle after miracle

What would you do if the United States Embassy official in Singapore denied you a student visa because you did not have a letter of job offer in the United States and Queenstown Baptist Church only had $11,000 in the bank? And yet within twenty-four hours, that very same official granted me a student visa, and welcomed Rose and me to the United States like we were long lost friends.

What would you do if an American missionary in Singapore told you that you should not go to America in December because there are no jobs in America in the month of December? How in the world would he know that?

When we arrived in our studio apartment at Golden Gate Seminary in Mill Valley, California, there were no light bulbs in our studio apartment on the first night at the seminary. I thought we were poor. The couple before us were worse off than we were. Would you believe that they left that studio apartment with all the light bulbs?

No wonder, my father told me not to be a pastor because most pastors are not only broke, but they also look broke! That night, Psalm 30:5 took on new meaning:

> "Weeping may linger for the night, but joy comes in the morning" (NRSV).

And yet within ten days of our arrival in the United States, God provided Rose a job to be the Pastor's secretary at the First Baptist Church in San Francisco, and I was invited to serve as the Youth Pastor at that same church.

We left Singapore for San Francisco with $1,000 in our pockets. The $1,000 paid for our studio apartment, tuition, transportation and food. Thankfully, we have a few more dollars today.

On January 2nd, 1978, the first day of my Preaching class at Golden Gate, Dr. J. P. Allen, my Preaching Professor, invited me to serve as his Graduate Assistant in Preaching during my two-and-one-half years of seminary studies. One of my responsibilities was to grade five hundred sermons every semester.

Four Timeless Lessons

Woven through the tapestry of my personal pilgrimage, four timeless lessons worth learning linger.

First, I want to live a life that is completely committed to Christ in obedience.

Second, every individual and church is important, but no individual or church is indispensable. Only Christ is. In a single significant statement Jesus declares:

> "Apart from Me you can do nothing" (John 15:5, AMP).

Third, Jesus Christ is the only One who can open doors for you. Listen to our living Lord as He speaks to your heart today:

> "Behold, I have set before you an open door, which no one is able to shut" (Revelation 3:8, RSV).

Fourthly and finally, I want to give my ministry skills, abilities, and experiences to the next generation of young people as they respond to God's call on their lives in ministry and mission on a global scale. God's work deserves my best. The incomparable hymn writer, Isaac Watts, writes as only he can:

> Love so amazing, so divine,
> Demands my soul, my life, my all.[92]

QBC's investment in the first eight years of my spiritual journey has reaped rich and rewarding dividends for the kingdom of God in Asia, Israel, and the United States.

You can take the boy out of QBC, but you will never be able to take QBC out of the boy!

> I know the Lord will make a way for me.
> I know the Lord will make a way for me.
> If I live a holy life, shun the wrong, and do the right.
> I know the Lord will make a way for me.[93]

15.

REJECTION ON THE MINISTRY JOURNEY

"Money and the Ministry Journey" is a vitally important subject to deal with if you are contemplating serving God in full-time ministry.

If "Money and the Ministry Journey" is first, "Rejection on the Ministry Journey" is a close second.

In fact, the earlier you grapple with rejection, the better off you'll be. This is not only informative, but it is also insightful.

When you are rejected, your world is reduced to something between depression and despair. That's why A. W. Tozer, one of my favorite devotional authors of yesteryear, notes:

> "It's doubtful God can use anyone greatly till he's hurt him deeply."[94]

Rejection in ministry takes many different forms. Stroll slowly with me as we consider some of them. Rejection is often necessary to prove the genuineness of your faith. At the same time, it teaches you humility.

Rejection could come when you choose to serve God in full-time ministry.

Rejection and God's Call

When I responded to God's call for full-time ministry in 1971, my mom called my grandma to inform her what I had decided to do. My grandma came with my uncle and his family to visit us. I vividly remember what my grandma did. She cupped my face in her hands and said, "That is a foolish thing you did."

By this time, I had already been walking with the Lord for five years. So my mind raced to what the apostle Paul says:

> "For the message of the cross is foolishness to those who are perishing, but to us who are being saved it is the power of God" (1 Corinthians 1:18, NIV).

No relative should stop you from fulfilling the plan and purpose of God in your life. This truth should give you hope beyond your rejection so that you see beyond your circumstance to your celestial calling.

Rejection and Relationships

Rejection can also come in the form of a boyfriend or girlfriend.

It is imperative that both of you share a similar calling as it relates to serving God in full-time ministry. In fifty years of ministry, Rose and I have witnessed too many divorces than we can count because such was not the case.

By the matchless mercy of God, you will find purpose in the scattering and sadness of your life. God still offers great grace for every shade of sorrow you have. Even though you cannot see Jesus in your rejection, He is there.

Rejection and Witnessing

Rejection may come when you share your faith with an unbeliever. Bill Bright, the Founder of Campus Crusade for Christ (now CRU) gives us a helpful definition:

> "Witnessing is sharing Christ in the power of the Holy Spirit and leaving the results to God."

Even as you strive to give an excellent explanation of the gospel, there will always be a few who will say "no." Even as you state your case for Christ intelligently and intelligibly with winsomeness and love, there will be a few who will say "no." Remember that people may be wooed to Christ, but not bullied to Him.

Sharing your faith with your family may be the most difficult but stay the course. I know, because after more than thirty years of witnessing, I had the joy of leading first, my father-in-law and then, my brother-in-law, to Christ.

Rejection and Fund Support

In over twenty years of raising significant sums of money for ministries, I have had my fair share of nos.

There are two things about no you need to know. Firstly, no does not mean no forever. Secondly, no is the beginning of yes.

With tenderness, Hudson Taylor writes:

> "It doesn't matter how great the pressure is; what really matters is where the pressure lies. Whether it comes between you and God or it presses you nearer His heart."[95]

My friend, God's plans for you are always the best. Don't try to grasp each thread of God's profound plan.

After you have been in the ministry for a few years, you will notice that the plans God has for you are full of surprises, with unexpected twists and abrupt turns. I can resonate with what a fellow pastor experienced:

> "One of the most frustrating things about Jesus is that … He is constantly moving us away from the places where we would prefer to stay … And moving us closer to … where we do not want to go."[96]

Jesus and Rejection

Peter, Christ's closest companion, deliberately denied Him when Jesus needed him the most.

Rejection is the experience of our Lord, and it shall be our experience as well. God is not going to replace suffering with glory; rather He will transform suffering into glory.[97]

If you are wondering what God is busy doing, He is busy shaping us into His image, and for me, He's got a long way to go.

If you walk with the author of your faith, you will never have to worry about the antagonist of your faith. As difficult as rejection is, it may be a painful page of your life; it is not the concluding chapter.

Is rejection causing you to have frightening fears and sleepless nights? Find comfort and consolation in the sacred Scripture that reminds us:

> "I will counsel you with My eye upon you" (Psalm 32:8, RSV).

That's why I love to sing those beautiful lyrics that Civilla D. Martin writes:

> His eye is on the sparrow,
> And I know He watches me.[98]

And the eye is closely connected to the mind. You are always on His mind. This gives you a reason to rejoice.

Dear sister and brother, remain courageous and committed in the face of rejection. Nothing compares with the joy of watching God step in and solve a problem that seems impossible. Andraé Crouch succinctly states:

> For if I'd never had a problem,
> I wouldn't know God could solve them.
> I'd never know what faith in God could do.[99]

16.

DEALING WITH DOUBTS ON THE JOURNEY

When God calls you to ministry, is it the thundering voice that shakes the earth or is it the still small voice of the Holy Spirit? You need to be cautious that the inner voice truly comes from God. But once you have confirmed that God has truly spoken to you, you need to obey God instantly and completely, no matter how ridiculous His command may seem.

Authentic Faith

Authentic faith often seems irrational and illogical. If you live your life according to common sense and logic, then you are not living by faith. Faith often defies logic or reason. Faith means stepping out and taking a risk.

Hebrews 11 tells us that Noah built an ark on dry land.

Abraham set out on a journey, not knowing where he was going.

Don't forget Moses who was raised in the household of Pharaoh to be a prince of Egypt. He chose to lead a nation of slaves out into the desert because God spoke to him from a burning bush.

It is audacious faith that is cautiously and carefully confirmed. Once you have carefully confirmed God's word to you, you will dare to do seemingly impossible things.

If you have faith, does it mean that you will not have doubts? No!

The Call of Jeremiah

Jeremiah was about thirty years old when God called him. Jesus was thirty old when he began His public ministry.

Jeremiah was acutely aware of his inadequacy and inexperience (Jeremiah 1:6). When Jeremiah told God that he was inadequate, God said:

> "You must go to everyone I send you to and say whatever I command you. Do not be afraid of them, for I am with you and will rescue you" (Jeremiah 1:7-8, NIV).

Do you worry that you lack eloquence and a strong speaking voice? Do you worry that you are too young and inexperienced for the challenge? Do you worry that you lack the courage and wisdom needed for the challenge?

God will be your voice. God will be your encourager. God will supply His wisdom. Whatever you need, He will give it to you.

Are you afraid you might appear foolish, that you might embarrass yourself? Well, I have done a royal job. Yet God worked through my weakness and foolishness, and He touched hearts with my tongue-tied speech.

Don't worry about making a fool of yourself. Be available and obedient for His purpose.

The Lord's message to Jeremiah is essentially the same promise He made before He ascended into heaven: "And surely, I am with you always, to the very end of the age" (Matthew 28:20, NIV).

It is God's own presence with us. It is God's own promise to us. It is the promise God made to Jeremiah: "Do not be afraid of them, for I am with you and will rescue you" (Jeremiah 1:8, NIV). The same promise of God that encouraged Jeremiah has also been delivered to us. As a result, when God calls us to a challenge, we should never say, "Lord, choose someone else. I'm inadequate to this challenge." Instead, we should say, "Yes, Lord. I know I can't do this in my strength but trusting in your promise to always be with me, I will obey you."

Next, notice the promise of power from God. This is a significant scene. "Then the LORD reached out his hand and touched my mouth and said to me, 'I have put my words in your mouth'" (Jeremiah 1:9, NIV).

In Isaiah 6, when God commissions the prophet to be His spokesman, Isaiah experiences majesty in the midst of the mundane.

> "Woe to me! I am ruined! For I am a man of unclean lips, and I live among a people of unclean lips, and my eyes have seen the King, the LORD Almighty" (Isaiah 6:5, NIV).

Then an angel flies to him with a hot coal in his hand and touches the burning coal to Isaiah's mouth, saying, "See, this has touched your lips; your guilt is taken away and your sin atoned for" (Isaiah 6:7, NIV).

In the same way, the Lord Himself reaches out and touches Jeremiah's mouth and says, "I have put my words in your mouth" (Jeremiah 1:9, NIV). The Lord's own words are the key to Jeremiah's power. Jeremiah now has on his lips the mighty power of the Word of God.

Faith and Doubts

Faith always has its doubts.

God works through our faith, so it should come as no surprise that the enemy of our souls seeks to attack our faith, and he does so by hurling doubts at us.

Let's not pretend that people of faith never doubt.

The Lord Jesus

Does it surprise you to know that our Lord Jesus Himself, though He lived by faith in everything He did, was sometimes subject to attacks of doubt? If that were not so, then the statement in Hebrews would not be true:

> "For we do not have a high priest who is unable to empathize with our weaknesses, but we have one who has been tempted in every way, just as we are – yet he did not sin" (Hebrews 4:15, NIV).

In the Garden of Gethsemane, Jesus doubted His mission. In the day, He had told His disciples that He had come to earth to die. But in that dark night, He experienced doubts about going through with that mission. He prayed three times that God would take the "cup" of the cross from Him (Matthew 26:36-46). And while He was on the cross, dying for our sins, He prayed: "My God, my God, why have you forsaken me?" (Psalm 22:1, NIV). This was a soul that was attacked by doubt!

God understands our doubts, and He accepts them. When we struggle and doubt, we should pray the prayer of the man who asked Jesus to heal his demon-possessed son: "I do believe; help me overcome my unbelief!" (Mark 9:24, NIV).

When Johnson Oatman, a Methodist minister, was in his mid-thirties, he wrote many gospel songs. In camp meetings across the United States, "Higher Ground" became a favorite. My desire is exquisitely expressed in these words:

> My heart has no desire to stay
> Where doubts arise and fears dismay;
> Though some may dwell where these abound,
> My prayer, my aim, is higher ground.[100]

17.

DEALING WITH EMOTIONS ON THE JOURNEY

In *The Road Less Traveled*, Scott Peck writes:

> "What makes life difficult is that the process of confronting and solving problems is a painful one … Yet it is in this whole process of meeting and solving problems that life has its meaning. Problems are the cutting edge that distinguishes between success and failure. Problems call forth our courage and wisdom; indeed, they create our courage and wisdom. It is only because of problems that we grow mentally and spiritually."[101]

Are you battle-weary from fighting enemies without and within? Do you feel abandoned, ridiculed, victimized? Your battle may be with a family member or a neighbor. It may be in your family, your home, or, of all places, in your church. Each is different, but all have a common element. You did what was right, you were acting upon your commitment to Christ, and yet the whole thing backfired!

David and Goliath

You will remember that David slew Goliath with a single stone from his sling (1 Samuel 17:49). But do you remember his eldest brother Eliab's reaction when he heard his youngest brother David ask about Goliath?

> "Why have you come down here? With whom did you leave those few sheep in the wilderness? I know your presumption (overconfidence) and the evil of your heart; for you have come down in order to see the battle" (1 Samuel 17:28, AMP).

How many times has that happened to you? Have you ever determined to do something important, only to have your closest relatives or friends doubt you?

The sad fact is that we can't always count on those we look up to for support.

Whenever you want to do something great for God, get ready for your brother or sister to give you all the reasons why you'll fail. Often the criticism comes from those who don't have the courage to accept the challenge themselves. Their thinking seems to be that if they're not going to succeed, they don't want anyone else to either.

Sometimes, your offer to help can be misunderstood, misconstrued and misrepresented. A ministry leader questions your motives.

My dear brother and sister, do not let anyone stop you from the divine destiny that God has particularly prepared for you alone.

Abraham Lincoln, raised poor and illiterate, was rebuffed by bankers, voters, employers, and law school deans before becoming president of the United States.

Thomas Edison's teachers told him he was too dumb to learn anything. He was also fired from his first two jobs.

Walt Disney was fired as a newspaper editor, with his boss saying he lacked imagination.

Colonel Sanders was told no 1,009 times by restaurant owners before he found one who would try his now-famous fried chicken recipe.

What's the Plan?

In such a difficult battle, the natural response by even the most godly person can be retaliation, revenge, or even rage. Such feelings are normal, even for Christians. But you do need a plan to handle your emotion because they can quickly tear you apart.

What are you to do with this ball of anger? Author Ross West offers this valuable advice:

> "Take it to the edge of the sea, place the ball in the hands of God, and let Him cast it as far as the east is from the west, so that it sinks into the depths, never to be seen or heard from again."[102]

Won't you place that ball in God's capable hands? In its place, He will give you a ball of joy.

From Paul's pen flows these words:

> "Nevertheless, you have done well to share with me in my difficulty. You yourselves also know, Philippians, that at the first preaching of the gospel, after I left Macedonia, no church shared with me in the matter of giving and receiving except you alone" (Philippians 4:14-15, NASB).

Paul's partners in Philippi carved a path of joy through the recording chambers of his memory. The words "joy" and "rejoice" are seamlessly woven through the tapestry of Philippians by silver threads and golden needles.

Those two words appear one-hundred-and-four times in Philippians. May I commend this book to you? This book of "joy" will bless you over and over again.

It continues to bless me today. God uses this book to fill my heart with joy as I serve Him.

He will do the same for you.

18.
DEALING WITH LOSS ON THE JOURNEY

Joe Bayly lost three of his children to death, two of them while they were teenagers. He later wrote a book, *The View from a Hearse*,[103] in which he talked about losing significant people. What a brutal, bruising blow!

The person you have lost might be a relative, a close friend or a colleague, and you are experiencing that loss alone. You may have lost that person either by death or by distance – either way, you've lost him. You've enjoyed his fellowship and companionship, and suddenly by death or by his moving away, you no longer have him near.

Bayly mentions in his book that one of the best contributions we can make to a person going through suffering and loss is our presence without words, not even verses of Scripture dumped on the ears of the grieving.

When you have friends who are going through the valley, they will appreciate the fact that you care. Your presence, some gracious act, a warm embrace – show that you care. In fact, just sitting beside them and crying with them often helps the most.

Have you recently suffered a loss? Maybe the wound is still tender; maybe it's too early to know why. You may never know why! But through it all, God has not left you.

Like a river rushing into a lake, the beautiful lyrics of "The Lily of the Valley" come to mind:

> In sorrow He's my comfort, in trouble He's my stay,
> He tells me ev'ry care on Him to roll.
>
> He will never, never leave me nor yet forsake me here,
> While I live by faith and do His blessed will. [104]

He is there all the time.

When His friend Lazarus was gravely ill, Lazarus' sisters sent messengers to Jesus to ask for help (John 11:1-3). But notice Jesus' response:

> "This sickness is not unto death, but for the glory of God, that the Son of God may be glorified through it" (John 11:4b).

Jesus' knowledge offers immeasurable comfort to the believer. Jesus knows the sword of sorrow that slices through our soul. He sees our suffering; even death does not escape His view. Remembering that we are safely in His sight reassures us that He cares.

Here's a song that encapsulates my thoughts exquisitely:

Who knows your disappointments?
Who hears each time you cry?
Who understands your heartaches?
Who dries the tears from your eyes?[105]

May I introduce you to "the Father of mercies and God of all comfort, who comforts us in all our affliction"? (2 Corinthians 1:3-4, NASB). His ability to comfort and console defies description.

It is remarkable how reassured I feel when the songwriter answers in the chorus:

Do you know my Jesus?
Do you know my friend?
Have you heard he loves you?
And that He will abide till the end?[106]

19.

A SONG FOR THE JOURNEY

Ira Stanphill was an accomplished musician and a minister with the Assemblies of God. He preached across America and in forty countries around the world.

Ira married Zelma Lawson, a minister's daughter. That marriage ended in a divorce. Sadly, Zelma died in an automobile accident.

Among the more than five hundred hymns he wrote are a few familiar favorites that you might know:

- There's Room at the Cross for You (1946)
- Mansion Over the Hilltop (1949)
- I Know Who Holds Tomorrow (1950)
- He Washed My Eyes with Tears (1955).

During the years of separation, divorce, and death, Ira sank into a deep depression. It was during those dark and difficult days that Ira wrote the lyrics to "I Know Who Holds Tomorrow."

One day he was driving when he began to hum and sing a song about not knowing what the future held but trusting God with the future. When he arrived home, he rushed to his office and his piano and jotted down these immortal words.

Out of his own personal blizzard blast of winter, Ira writes words that are nothing short of phenomenal. With poetic eloquence, evangelist Stanphill writes from the depths of his own personal pain and loss:

> I don't know about tomorrow.
> I just live from day to day.
> I don't borrow from its sunshine,
> For its skies may turn to grey.
> I don't worry o'er the future,
> For I know what Jesus said.
> And today I'll walk beside Him,
> For He knows what is ahead.
>
> Many things about tomorrow,
> I don't seem to understand.
> But I know who holds tomorrow,
> And I know who holds my hand.[107]

What was he thinking about when he said:

> Many things about tomorrow,
> I don't seem to understand.[108]

Ira is not alone in making this claim.

Dr. Li Yung Hua

I listened intently to a moving testimony from the worship leader at Cherith Baptist Church in Singapore. Prior to leading the congregation in singing, my friend and brother mentioned that this song holds special meaning for him. For a period of time in 2020, he was lethargic, short of breath. He did not know why. His wife encouraged him to see his cardiologist friend.

Dr. Li Yung Hua, the renowned orthopedic and spine surgeon, discovered that his main artery was ninety-five percent blocked. They call it "the widow-maker." A surgical procedure saved his life.

Because of the "Goodness of God,"[109] Dr. Li is deeply grateful that it is by God's grace that he is still alive and that he is given a second chance to serve Him. Dr. and Mrs. Li have three adult children who are in the medical profession.

In your dungeon of discouragement, may you discover that the One who comes to you is still the One who takes you from your dungeon to your destiny. Then will arise within you splashing streams of hope.

Even though "God doesn't promise us tomorrow, he does promise us eternity,"[110] said Tony Snow, an American journalist who died of cancer in 2008.

20.

ENCOURAGEMENT FOR THE JOURNEY

Question: Who needs encouragement? Answer: Everyone who breathes.

No truer words than these have been spoken by actress Celeste Holms when she said: "We live by encouragement and we die without it."[111]

I believe it was writer Christopher Morley who says that if everybody has only five minutes to live, each would be sending out final words of affection and affirmation.[112] I do not want to wait until that time comes.

I cannot thank God enough for forty-six years with Rose, the darling and delight of my life, two precious sons, Joshua, and Jonathan; two "perfect" grandsons, Josiah and Caleb; many miles traveled, and mistakes made and forgiven.

Rose has typed everything I have written either on a typewriter, a word processor or a computer. In short, if she did not type all my long research papers in Bible College, seminary, and doctoral work, I'd still be in college! She also typed notes from the thousands of books I have read since we were dating.

One of the things that I least enjoyed doing in ministry was going to Board meetings. How did I get through them? She prayed me through every one of them.

What an essential role Rose's encouragement plays in my life. Because of her encouragement, I may be exhausted yet exuberant.

What Ralph Waldo Emerson said of enthusiasm can also be said of encouragement: "Nothing great can ever be achieved without enthusiasm."[113]

I don't know about you. I am motivated by encouragement. I count on it. I fail without it. Leadership in the ministry demands it. Projects are completed because of it. Responsibilities become grim and grinding assignments without the relief that encouragement provides.

I am persuaded that one of the reasons God gives us so many personal promises in His sacred Scriptures is to encourage us.

Knowledge is essential – but knowledge without encouragement is like saying "thank you" to your ministry partners without a smile. Those who encourage others in private as consistently as they do in public are not only rare, but they are also remarkable.

I submit to you that without Barnabas, "the son of encouragement" (Acts 4:36-37), there would not have been a John Mark (Acts 15:37-39). Notice that the names were switched from "Barnabas ... and Saul" (Acts 13:1) to "Paul and Barnabas" (Acts 13:42). Without Barnabas, there would not have been an Apostle Paul (Acts 9:27-28, cf. 2 Timothy 4:11). "Paul owed more to Barnabas than to any other man."[114] Without Barnabas, we would not have half of the New Testament!

Do you know of someone who should be promoted to a place of prominence, and is presently in need of your companionship and confidence?

Someday soon you might be the one in need of encouragement. How, then, do you dispense encouragement? What Samuel Johnson commented is worth considering: "When a man knows he is to be hanged in a fortnight, it concentrates his mind wonderfully."[115]

Think of one person you know who could really use a word of support. Then give it! Don't just think about it. Do it. Do it today!

Pray for that individual you were thinking about. Ask God to give you just the right word, just the right method of approaching that person. Maybe you need to write a note. Maybe you need to make a phone call. Maybe you need to take the person out for a cup of coffee or invite him or her over for a meal.

That may be just the encouragement that person needs.

In choosing our words carefully, Dan Allender and Tremper Longman say in stunning simplicity: "We are to speak words of encouragement to draw forth the heart of God in those we love."[116]

21.
OBEDIENCE ON THE JOURNEY

Speaking about the baptism of Jesus, Philip Keller writes,

> "When the day came for Jesus to gently close the door to His carpenter shop for the last time, He knew exactly where to go. With firm footsteps and quiet determination, He set off directly to see John. Following the winding roads from the hill country of Nazareth, He headed down into the burning heat of the Jordan Valley where John was baptizing in the running river."[117]

Edging His way through the crowd, Jesus silently slipped off His sandals and eased into the murky river to be baptized by John. It was late in the day and many had already been baptized when Jesus stepped into the water (Luke 3:21).

Mark records Jesus' baptism thus:

> "And immediately coming up out of the water, He saw the heavens opening, and the Spirit like a dove descending upon Him" (Mark 1:10, NASB).

Jesus Prayed and Holy Spirit Descended

Luke describes the same event in his gospel, but he adds an element that Mark leaves out. As Jesus emerged from the water, He was talking to His Father.

> "And while He was praying, heaven was opened, and the Holy Spirit descended upon Him in bodily form like a dove" (Luke 3:21-22, NASB).

Luke is also more specific than Mark when he describes the dove. This dove was not merely a symbol of the Holy but actually was the Holy Spirit in bodily form.

God Spoke

Imagine John the Baptist's astonishment as he saw the heavens parting, the Son of God praying, the Holy Spirit descending and God the Father speaking:

> "And a voice came out of heaven, 'You are My beloved Son, in You I am well-pleased'" (Luke 3:22, NASB).

Jesus' baptism came at the right time, in the right way, and for the right reason. Listen to what Jesus says to John:

> "Permit it at this time; for in this way it is fitting for us to fulfill all righteousness" (Matthew 3:15, NASB).

These three phrases "at this time," "in this way" and "to fulfill all righteousness" are three timeless truths of God's unusual plans for you and me.

So let's look at these three powerful principles so that we may obey.

"At This Time"

The Lord's timing sometimes seems beyond reason, but if we could only see things from His perspective, we would understand that it's divinely precise.

Paul says that "when the fullness of time had come, God sent forth His Son" (Galatians 4:4, NKJV). The Greek word here is "Kairos," meaning God's "right time" (NLT).

So when God calls you into full-time ministry, He calls you clearly and calmly in the "Kairos" moment of your life.

Are you feeling the prompting and prodding of the Holy Spirit? Maybe from your perspective, the timing might be off, but from God's viewpoint, the timing is perfect. "Permit" God's perfect timing to work in your life, and you will find as I did, that the Lord will be glorified.

"When the right time comes, I will make this happen quickly. I am the LORD!" (Isaiah 60:22, GNB).

"In This Way"

The preeminent prophet in the Old Testament says:

> "For my thoughts are not your thoughts, neither are your ways my ways," declares the LORD. "As the heavens are higher than the earth, so are my ways higher than your ways, and my thoughts than your thoughts" (Isaiah 55:8-9, NIV).

Sometimes God's ways of doing things don't seem to make sense. Does shouting at a wall make it crumble? It does if it's the wall of Jericho.

Every barren woman would understand Sarah's silent sorrow as time erased her hopes of pregnancy. But the LORD announced:

> "At the appointed time I will return to you, at this time next year, Sarah will have a son" (Genesis 18:14, NASB).

Do ninety-year-old women have babies? There was one who did. Sarah is her name.

Sarah and her husband waited for twenty-five years for Isaac to be born.

Does our Savior need to be baptized? The Son of God did. It was the right way for Jesus' ministry to begin.

This may be the opportunity for you to do something extraordinary for God. Proceed in God's time, do it in God's way, and leave the results to Him.

"To Fulfill All Righteousness"

When you respond to God's call on your life with obedience, you are inextricably interconnected to Him in the eternal work of righteousness. This partnership may take you into uncharted territory, but the assurance of Christ's presence will give you the courage to press on. I promise you on the authority of God's Word that in those lonely moments, He will take care of your needs. He will replace your fear with faith.

Although Habakkuk faced his future with fear, he mustered a remarkable faith in God. Listen as he expressed his fears:

> "Though the fig tree does not blossom
> And there is no fruit on the vines,
> Though the yield of the olive fails
> And the fields produce no food,
> Though the flock is cut off from the fold
> And there are no cattle in the stalls ..." (Habakkuk 3:17, AMP).

Habakkuk replaced his fear with faith. How? Instead of looking back or looking around, he looked up. What follows this list of woes, is a breathtakingly beautiful statement of trust in God:

> "Yet I will [choose to] rejoice in the LORD;
> I will [choose to] shout in exultation in the [victorious] God of my salvation!
> The Lord God is my strength [my source of courage, my invincible army];
> He has made my feet [steady and sure] like hinds' feet
> And makes me walk [forward with spiritual confidence] on my high places [of challenge and responsibility]" (Habakkuk 3:18-19, AMP).

Your part is to respond to God without reservation. You don't have to be creative or clever. All you have to do is to trust and obey.

The real work begins here – with your obedience: "Behold, to obey is better than sacrifice" (1 Samuel 15:22, RSV). This was the first verse I learned in Sunday school so many years ago.

> Trust and obey,
> For there's no other way
> To be happy in Jesus,
> But to trust and obey.[118]

Jesus obediently walked up Mount Calvary to the cross. We can't know all the reasons that our Father is allowing bad things to happen to us, but like Jesus, we can trust Him in those difficult times. As we look at Him and rejoice in what He did for us, we can follow the call of God when times seem the darkest and most difficult.

22.

LIVING OUT YOUR CONVICTIONS ON THE JOURNEY

Only God knows what treacherous times lay ahead for us. That's why He is looking for leaders who have depth of convictions. Phyllis Thompson, in her book, *D. E. Hoste*, writes:

> "I suppose if you really want to know who is a spiritual leader, you ought to look around and see how many who are spiritual are following him."[119]

G. K. Chesterton asserts that it is not the one with convictions who is out of touch, it is the rest of the world. He observes:

> "The Christian ideal … has not been tried and found wanting; it has been found difficult and left untried."[120]

What tough times require is an intensity of devotion. It was Sir Winston Churchill, in the midst of Nazi bombings, who said to the people of London:

> "This is not the end. It is not even the beginning of the end. But it is, perhaps, the end of the beginning."[121]

This is evidenced in the depth of convictions. According to J. Oswald Sanders:

> "A small man may entertain strong opinions; a great man cherishes strong convictions. Opinions cost only breath. Convictions may well cost blood."[122]

Jim Elliott

Jim Elliott was murdered while attempting to communicate the gospel to the aggressive Auca Indians in Ecuador. Yet, through the tunnel of time since his untimely death, his words still reverberate.

> "He is no fool who gives what he cannot keep to gain what he cannot lose."[123]

It all boils down to this: Do you really believe what you say you believe?

D. L. Moody

If there was one person who inspired me more than any other, it had to be pastor and evangelist Dwight Lyman Moody, better known as D. L. Moody.

There was probably no better shoe salesman in Chicago than Moody in the 1850's. But Moody felt God's call to leave his thriving shoe business and go into full-time ministry. It was not an easy decision. Listen to Moody in his own words: "I fought against it. It was a terrible battle."[124]

It meant spending all his savings, living on crackers and cheese, rooming at the YMCA, and putting off marriage. He wrestled with God's call for three sleepless months.

Here's the rest of the story. Moody resigned his sales job. By the time he was twenty-three, his Sunday school class had grown to over fifteen hundred children. Five years later he became the President of the YMCA. And, by the time Moody was fifty, this "uneducated" preacher had founded a church, a Bible Institute, and rocked two continents for Christ.

My Personal Testimony[125]

As for me, One greater than Moses spoke to me in September 1971 from His wonderful Word:

> "If anyone serves me, he must follow me; and where I am, there shall my servant be also; if anyone serves me, the Father will honor him" (John 12:26, RSV).

How did I come to read that passage that day? I was reading a chapter a day. For nine months, I had been resisting God's call on my life. For nine months, I had said, "No."

Like Jacob, I was so tired of wrestling with God. Finally, I said, "God, you have one shot. If you want me to serve You in ministry, then You'll need to speak to me from Your Word tonight, not tomorrow."

The night before, I was reading John 11. So that night, I turned to John 12. John 12 always follows John 11.

As with Moses, the fire of God burned out all my excuses.

Are you wrestling with God's call on your life right now? This is God's word for you:

> "My grace is sufficient for you, for My strength is made perfect in weakness" (2 Corinthians 12:9, NKJV).

Do you dare to live out your convictions? What are you waiting for?

Ann Wells wrote a thought-provoking article in the *Los Angeles Times*. What a refreshing and reassuring reminder!

> "Don't ever save anything for a special occasion. Everyday you're alive is a special occasion."[126]

Every day you and I are alive is a special occasion.

Your story waits to be told.

23.
THE LOVE OF GOD ON THE JOURNEY

"You are nobody till somebody loves you,"[127] goes the popular song. Our contemporary culture has taken it literally. So, we celebrate it in a song. Hence, we are disappointed and disillusioned because we have misplaced our hopes for happiness on romantic relationships, on human affirmation and acceptance that only God can provide. "This is a miniature of our disillusionment, experienced from Eden onwards."[128] Instead, we should reorient our focus toward God and His love.

The words of Paul come to mind. He commences by saying that "there is now no condemnation for those who are in Christ Jesus" (Romans 8:1, AMP), and concludes by saying that:

> "Nothing can ever separate us from God's love. Neither death nor life, neither angels nor demons, neither our fears for today nor our worries about tomorrow – not even the powers of hell can separate us from God's love. No power in the sky above or in the earth below – indeed, nothing in all creation will be able to separate us from the love of God that is revealed in Christ Jesus our Lord" (Romans 8:38-39, NLT).

Nothing can destroy it, defile it, diminish it, or displace it. Isn't it a great relief? No disorder, no disease, not even death itself can separate us from the love of God.

Frederick M. Lehman encapsulates the essence of what I want to say about the love of God:

> Could we with ink the ocean fill,
> And were the skies of parchment made;
> Were every stalk on earth a quill,
> And every man a scribe by trade;
> To write the love of God above
> Would drain the ocean dry;
> Nor could the scroll contain the whole,
> Though stretched from sky to sky.
>
> Oh, love of God, how rich and pure!
> How measureless and strong!
> It shall forevermore endure
> The saints' and angels' song.[129]

God reaches out to us in spite of our brokenness and baggage. This is not a New Testament concept.

There's an incredible verse in Deuteronomy that explains why God loves us so much. From the mouth of Moses comes these words:

> "The Lord did not set his heart on you and choose you because you were more numerous than other nations, for you were the smallest of all nations! Rather, it was simply that the Lord loves you" (Deuteronomy 7:7-8, NLT).

Why does God love you? Not because you are bigger or better than anyone else, but simply because He loves you.

The great Bible teacher, G. Campbell Morgan says:

> "There is a text that I have never attempted to preach on, though I have gone around it and around it – John 3:16. It is too big. When I have read it, there is nothing else to say."[130]

The Prodigal Son

God is like the father in the story of the prodigal son (Luke 15:11-32). The son had the dubious distinction of making a wreck and waste of his own life. An ungrateful son took the inheritance his father gave him and squandered it in a far country. In his brokenness, as he ate the same filthy food he fed to the pigs, the son remembered his father and the home he had left behind. C. S. Lewis puts it beautifully when he writes:

> "God whispers to us in our pleasures, speaks in our conscience, but shouts in our pains; it is His megaphone to rouse a deaf world."[131]

In the story Jesus told, the father watches the horizon day after day, hoping to see his wandering son return. That is a portrait of the heart of God, who patiently and persistently pleads for His children to return to Him and to the protective everlasting embrace of His loving arms.

The father let the prodigal son go, but love demanded that the father always be ready with open arms should the son ever return. When the father saw his son in the distance, he ran to greet him with open arms – ready to receive him and restore him.

God has promised that if we return to Him, He will forgive us and rebuild our broken lives.

Someone else's action cannot dictate our response. God sent His Son into a world that hated Him. If God had waited for the world to be "worthy" to receive Him, His Son would never have come.

In matchless words, evangelist William Bell Riley observed:

> "It was … in search of souls, that caused Christ to be crucified, and the same fact caused the great apostle Paul to be imprisoned. But without it there could have been no Christian church, no soul-winning endeavor worthy the name."[132]

In bold moves and with courageous actions, Jesus loved in the days He walked on earth – Judas, the woman at the well, Zacchaeus, and many others like them. In spite of the fact that Jesus was without sin and these people were very much steeped in sin, Jesus still honored them. He washed Judas' feet. He spent time talking respectfully to the woman at the well. He went to Zacchaeus' home for dinner. Jesus, the only perfect human being to live on this earth, moved toward sinful people.

A New Commandment

Jesus asks us to do the same. Ponder His commandment in John 13:34-35 put in a moving melody:

A new commandment I give unto you:
That you love one another as I have loved you,
That you love one another as I have loved you.

By this shall all men know that you are My disciples,
If you have love one for one another.
By this shall all men know that you are My disciples,
If you have love one for one another.[133]

"No one is of the Spirit of Christ but he that has the utmost compassion for sinners."[134] That is why Katherine Anne Porter eloquently explains:

> "Love must be learned, and learned again and again; there is no end to it. Hate needs no instruction, but waits only to be provoked."[135]

That is what God is saying to us when He says, "I have loved you with an everlasting love" (Jeremiah 31:3, NASB). He is saying that His love for us surpasses our comprehension. It transcends our imagination.

How does Paul speak of God's love?

> "And I pray that you, being rooted and established in love, may have power, together with all the Lord's holy people, to grasp how wide and long and high and deep is the love of Christ, and to know this love that surpasses knowledge—that you may be filled to the measure of all the fullness of God" (Ephesians 3:17-19, NIV).

In short, God loves us with an everlasting love, a love that is wider and longer and higher and deeper than we can possibly imagine.

There will be times when we are tempted to think that God is unjust or uncaring or unloving. But God wants us to understand that the things that happen in our lives don't always feel warm and pleasant, yet God has loved us with an everlasting love. The Christian life is a journey of learning to trust His love even in painful circumstances.

When was the last time you looked back over your life and counted up the ways God has demonstrated His providential love for you? We tend to take God's blessings for granted. We are far more focused on what we don't have than what we do have. We have bought into the fear that we are missing out, the fear that we don't have enough stuff, the narcissistic notion that we deserve more and more stuff.

Have you thanked God for the victories He has achieved in your life? Have you thanked Him for the promotions you didn't expect to get? For the blessings you didn't deserve? For the consequences and punishment you should have received that God spared you from?

That, my brothers and sisters, is the love of God. The great Scottish preacher, Alexander Whyte, puts it in these forceful words: "Till Christ came, no soul was ever made such a battleground between heaven and earth"[136] as yours and mine were. That's why "... in all these things we are more than conquerors through Him who loved us" (Romans 8:37, NKJV).

24.

GOD'S GRACE FOR THE JOURNEY

Mickey Cohen was a notorious crime boss. He was a violent man who had killed countless people, and he was living in an armed fortress in Brentwood, California.

Billy Graham explained the gospel to Cohen, and the crime boss said he wanted to receive Christ. But within days, it became clear that Cohen had not altered his lifestyle in the slightest. He was still living a life of crime. Dr. Graham explained to Cohen that he could not follow Christ and continue his criminal career. He had to repent of his crimes.

Cohen was shocked. "Why do I have to give up my career? There are movie stars, Christian athletes, Christian businessmen. So why not a Christian gangster? If that's Christianity, count me out."[137]

In our decaying and darkening culture, this understanding of God's grace is finite and fragmentary. Only the wisdom of God's Word can free us from the mud, muck, and mire of our own fallen flesh.

Romans 6

As I graze gently in this liberating letter, I realize that Romans 6 is not easy and entertaining. In his magnificent magna carta, Paul asks:

> "What shall we say, then? Shall we go on sinning so that grace may increase?" (Romans 6:1, NIV).

He emphatically exclaims: "By no means!" (Romans 6:2, NIV).

To Martyn Lloyd-Jones grace was not only risky, it was downright dangerous. He was clearly convinced it could be easily misunderstood.[138]

In *The Cost of Discipleship*, Dietrich Bonhoeffer called this "cheap grace." He writes with startling clarity:

> "Cheap grace is the preaching of forgiveness without requiring repentance, baptism without church discipline, Communion without confession … Cheap grace is grace without discipleship, grace without the cross, grace without Jesus Christ, living and incarnate."[139]

Cheap grace takes a diminished view of the awfulness of sin and a diminished view of the holiness and justice of God.

The way to return to God is to acknowledge our guilt. As long as our sin remains unacknowledged and unconfessed, we cannot return to God. We need to take sin as seriously as He does.

God extends grace to us. He invites us to come home with Him as He adopts us into His forever family.

Now, consider two magnificent models of grace – Paul and Jesus.

Paul and Grace

Paul, the prolific preacher of grace, appreciated grace more than any other. Carefully consider the testimony of a proud persecutor-turned-preacher. I pause periodically at this section of Scripture:

> "After that He appeared to more than five hundred brothers and sisters at one time, the majority of whom are still alive, but some have fallen asleep [in death]. Then He was seen by James, then by all the apostles, and last of all, as to one untimely (prematurely, traumatically) born, He appeared to me also. For I am the least [worthy] of the apostles, and not fit to be called an apostle, because I [at one time] fiercely oppressed and violently persecuted the church of God. But by the [remarkable] grace of God I am what I am, and His grace toward me was not without effect. In fact, I worked harder than all of the apostles, though it was not I, but the grace of God [His unmerited favor and blessing which was] with me. So whether it was I or they, this is what we preach, and this is what you believed and trusted in and relied on with confidence" (1 Corinthians 15:9-11, AMP).

This scripture is helpful. Paul writes clearly and candidly of his own track record. After listing the apostles whom the risen Lord appeared to, he states, "last of all … He appeared to me also." Notice how Paul refers to himself with exquisite eloquence: "as to one untimely [prematurely, traumatically] born."

As if that is not enough, Paul sees himself "as the least [worthy] of the apostles." He refused to compare himself to or compete with his contemporaries. I love the way one commentary puts it:

> "In spite of his unfitness to bear the name, the grace of God has made him equal to it. The persecutor has been forgiven and the abortion adopted."[140]

This is nothing short of remarkable.

This is why Paul amplifies the scriptural statement in Romans 5:20. Where sin measurably increased, grace immeasurably increased. Where sin abounds, grace superabounds. Jesus' death on the cross was the sufficient payment for our sin. His grace was not only adequate, it was abundant. That's all any of us can claim:

> Nothing in my hands I bring,
> Simply to Thy cross I cling.[141]

Jesus and Grace

When Jesus told stories, grace was his favorite theme. Did you notice that He has a gracious way of handling children? Even though the Prodigal Son had a dubious distinction of making a wreck and waste of his life, Jesus spoke of him with grace. When He told the story of the Good Samaritan, grace abounded. Christ smiled with favor on the unnamed sinner who said: "God, be merciful to me, a sinner!" (Luke 18:13, RSV). Remember His prayer from the cross: "Father, forgive them, for they do not know what they do" (Luke 23:34, NKJV). Amazing, this grace!

When we bless the Lord on our journey, we realize that it's not about us; it's about God's great grace.

David was Israel's greatest king, yet he committed adultery and premeditated murder to cover up his carefully concealed sin. But the New Testament calls David a "man after My own heart" (Acts 13:22, NIV).

The same is true of Abraham. He had many failings of faith. His tryst with Hagar to hurry along God's promise. His pawning of Sarah as his sister to save his own skin. And yet when the New Testament speaks of Abraham, it highlights the triumphs of his faith, and not the tragedy of his failures (Romans 4:18-21).

In the gallery of faith, we see priceless pictures of flawed people like Noah, Moses, Jacob, and Samson. Although there are dark and distorted pictures in each of their lives, the writer of Hebrews chooses to focus on their faith (Hebrews 11). That's the good news of God's great grace!

Any person who is greatly used of God is a recipient of God's great grace. A. W. Tozer, the devotional author, notes: "It is doubtful God can use anyone greatly till he's hurt him deeply."[142] God, in His matchless mercy, has chosen to give great grace to imperfect, ill-deserving individuals like us. Grace that is magnificent beyond belief.

Amazing Grace

From the belly of the ship, John Newton, the slave owner, could hear the slaves from West Africa singing. In 1772, he wrote the lyrics of this stirring and soaring spiritual that has taken on new meaning for me.

Amazing grace how sweet the sound
That saved a wretch like me.
I once was lost, but now am found
Was blind, but now I see.

'Twas grace that taught my heart to fear
And grace my fears relieved
How precious did that grace appear?
The hour I first believed.[143]

Chris Tomlin and Pastor Louie Giglio co-wrote this chorus:

My chains are gone, I've been set free.
My God, my Savior has ransomed me
And like a flood, His mercy reigns,
Unending love,
Amazing grace.[144]

These lyrics are reminiscent of eighteenth-century British evangelist Charles Wesley's powerful and joyful hymn. Wesley wrote:

Long my imprisoned spirit lay
Fast bound in sin and nature's night.
Thine eye diffused a quick'ning ray:
I woke, the dungeon flamed with light!
My chains fell off, my heart was free;
I rose, went forth and followed Thee.[145]

We were trapped in a dark dungeon of despair. Jesus extended to us unexpected, undeserved and unearned grace. He freed us by breaking the bars of sin and shame.

Salvation is by grace alone, and living the Christian life is also by grace alone. James makes the definitive declaration about the believer's experience:

> "But He gives us more and more grace [through the power of the Holy Spirit to defy sin and live an obedient life that reflects both our faith and our gratitude for our salvation"] (James 4:6, AMP).

This is not saving grace, but grace to live our lives as we ought in this fallen world. Thank God – daily He gives us an extra measure of His grace.

This leads to one conclusion. We all need the grace of God. Says John Blanchard:

> "For daily need there is daily grace; for sudden need, sudden grace; for overwhelming need, overwhelming grace."[146]

When George MacDonald, the great Scottish preacher, was talking with his son about the glories of the future, his son interrupted and said, "It seems too good to be true, Daddy." MacDonald answered, "Nay, laddy, it is just so good it must be true!"[147]

God's great grace is almost too good to be true. It is God's great grace from beginning to end.

25.

GOD'S MERCY ON THE JOURNEY

Mephibosheth is a grandson of King Saul (2 Samuel 4:4). Crippled and forgotten, he lived a life of obscurity in a place called "Lodebar," translated means "a place of barrenness." One day, in his prosperity, David remembers his friend Jonathan. He asks and is told that:

> "There is still a son of Jonathan who is crippled in both feet" (2 Samuel 9:1-3, NASB).

David not only shows Mephibosheth mercy, but on four separate times in this biblical account we read that the cripple would eat at the king's table – verses 7, 10, 11, and finally verse 13:

> "So Mephibosheth lived in Jerusalem, for he ate at the king's table regularly. Now he was lame in both his feet" (2 Samuel 9:13, NASB).

David shows grace to one who does not deserve it and can never earn it. In the words of the famed pastor-preacher, Donald Grey Barnhouse, of the Tenth Presbyterian Church in Philadelphia, Pennsylvania, this is "love that stoops."[148]

This is a powerful picture of God's mercy coming over us like a soft-falling rain that washes away our sadness and sorrow. By His unfailing mercy, "fresh as the morning, as sure as the sunrise" (Lamentations 3:22-23, GNT), we can find purpose on the picturesque paths of our lives. Mercy that we do not deserve and have no right to demand and can only receive.

In one of the great speeches in Shakespeare's *The Merchant of Venice*, Portia persuasively pleads for mercy:

> "The quality of mercy is not strained.
> It droppeth as the gentle rain from heaven
> Upon the place beneath.
> It is twice blessed –
> It blesseth him that gives, and him that takes."[149]

That's why in Jeremiah's journal he reminds us that "God's mercies are new every morning" (Lamentations 3:23, ESV).

I love the lines from that old hymn, "Day by Day":

> Ev'ry day the Lord Himself is near me
> With a special mercy for each hour.
> All my cares He fain would bear, and cheer me,
> He whose name is Counselor and Pow'r.[150]

Mysteriously, yet magnificently, God's mercy brings the relief that you and I so desperately need today. He has more mercy than we have misery.

God, who has every reason to judge us for our iniquities, graciously grants us His mercy. In a previous generation, William Newell reminds us:

> Mercy there was great, and grace was free,
> Pardon that was multiplied to me.[151]

And when we lay our sins before Him, He cleanses us. We can no longer keep our feelings from the sharp, searching gaze of our King. As His children, He gives us a purity that matches His own, and then we can fellowship with Him (1 John 1:7).

And His tablecloth covers our feet.

26.

A CALL TO PURITY ON THE JOURNEY

Prior to his adulterous affair with Bathsheba, David was a success story (2 Samuel 5-11). He was at the zenith of his career. Afterwards, everything goes downhill. Defeat on the battlefield. His baby died. His beautiful daughter, Tamar, was raped by her half-brother, Amnon. Amnon was murdered by Tamar's full-brother Absalom. Absalom came to so hate his father David for his moral turpitude that he led a rebellion under the tutelage of Bathsheba's resentful grandfather, Ahithophel. David ultimately dies heartbroken, his family in disarray and his successor son, Solomon, primed for an even greater fall.

Vulnerable after Victory

The unvarnished, untarnished, and unmitigated truth is that we are most vulnerable after victory. David is fresh off a series of great victories on the battlefield. 2 Samuel 11:1 opens the scene with these picturesque words:

> "Then it happened in the spring, at the time when the kings go out to battle, that David sent Joab … and all [the fighting men of] Israel, and they destroyed the Ammonites and besieged Rabbah. But David remained in Jerusalem" (AMP).

David was in bed, not in battle. He belonged in the battle; instead, he was in the bedroom. J. Oswald Sanders sums it up succinctly: "David's greatest fault lay in his yielding to passions of the flesh."[152]

"But"

Was it William Shakespeare who said that "but" is the most important word in the English language? The word "but" is petite but potent. Instead of being in battle, David was enjoying the sights and sound of the evening sunset. Verse 2 records:

> "One evening David got up from his couch and was walking on the [flat] roof of the king's palace, and from there he saw a woman bathing; and she was very beautiful in appearance" (AMP).

It had been a warm day, and evening was falling. The king strode out on the rooftop for some cool air and a look at his city at dusk. As he gazed, his eye caught the form of an unusually beautiful woman who was bathing. The Hebrew was explicit in this verse: the woman was "beautiful of appearance, very."

David looked at her. His look became a sinful stare, and then a libidinous leer.

Notice that the Bible says: "David took" (verse 4).

The Progression of Sin

David saw. David coveted. David took. David hid. That's the progression of sin. It was true of Adam and Eve (Genesis 3:6-8). It was true of Achan (Joshua 7:20-21). It was certainly true of David here.

Dietrich Bonhoeffer wisely writes about temptation. Like David, you and I wrestle with it. "All at once a secret smoldering fire is kindled. The flesh burns and is in flames."[153]

And when the flame of lust is fanned,

> "God is quite unreal to us … He loses all reality, and only desire for the creature is real … Satan does not here fill us with hatred of God, but with forgetfulness of God. The lust thus aroused envelopes the mind and will of man in deep darkness. The powers of clear discrimination and decision are taken from us."[154]

What a world of wisdom there is in these statements. When we are in the grip of lust, the reality of God fades. The longer king David leered; the less real God became to him. Not only was his awareness of God diminished, but David lost awareness of who he was – his holy call, and the certain consequences of sin. This is what lust does! It has done it millions of times. God disappears to lust-glazed eyes.

"Run!"

That's why when the New Testament lingers on the lure and lair of lurid lust, it gives us one clear command: "Run from anything that stimulates youthful lusts" (2 Timothy 2:22, NLT). In short, run from any satisfying stimulation.

If you do not run, you will fall. If you try to fight it, you will fall. This is the only counsel that works for you and me.

Now, back to the story.

Second Look

Not only did David take a second look, but he leered for an undetermined period of time. Fueled by lust, he envisioned the pleasure of sex with that beautiful woman. Burned and blinded by desire for Bathsheba, he wanted, rather, he coveted her. Then, "David sent word and inquired about the woman" (2 Samuel 11:3a, AMP).

When his intent became apparent to his servants, one tried to dissuade him, saying, "Is this not Bathsheba, the daughter of Eliam, the wife of Uriah the Hittite?" (2 Samuel 11:3b, AMP). That significant statement was couched in the form of a question. Embedded in that question to the king was a warning of wisdom. It was not even subtle. Simply put, "The woman's married."

But David would not be rebuffed. A massive rationalization took place in David's mind as J. Allan Peterson suggests:

> "Uriah is a great soldier but he's probably not much of a husband or a lover – years older than she is – and he'll be away for a long time. This girl needs a little comfort in her

> loneliness. This is one way I can help her. No one will get hurt. I do not mean anything wrong by it. This is not lust – I have known that many times. This is love. This is not the same as finding a prostitute on the street. God knows that. And to the servant, 'Bring her to me.'"[155]

It is amazing how the mind controlled by lust has an infinite capacity for rationalization.

At that single moment in time God was, in the words of Bonhoeffer, "quite unreal" to David. His desire for sexual pleasure with Bathsheba was primary and paramount. He ignored his servant's warning and the catastrophic consequences that would follow.

> "David sent messengers and took her. When she came to him, he lay with her. And when she was purified from her uncleanness, she returned to her house" (2 Samuel 11:4, AMP).

"Passing Pleasures"

The writer of Hebrews calls this "the passing pleasures of sin" (Hebrews 11:25, NASB, AMP). The "pleasures of sin" are fleeting. They are temporal, transitory, temporary. They are enjoyable, but they are "passing." They don't last. And when they vanish, as they surely will, they leave behind a river of regret.

The "passing pleasures of sin" are enjoyable but they are "for a season" (KJV). For David, the pleasure is gone in a matter of weeks, because Bathsheba "sent word and told David, 'I am pregnant'" (2 Samuel 11:5, AMP).

The record of the tragic fall of king David should be taken seriously by the Church of Jesus Christ. It is meant not only to instruct us, but to frighten us – to scare the sensuality out of us!

Outcome

In the words of Pastor F. B. Meyer, David's outcome is succinctly stated:

> "One brief spell of passionate indulgence, and then—his character blasted irretrievably; his peace vanished; the foundation of his kingdom imperiled; the Lord displeased; and great occasion given to his enemies to blaspheme!"[156]

The Call to Purity

The most explicit call to sexual purity is found in 1 Thessalonians 4:3-8:

> "It is God's will that you should be *holy*; that you should avoid sexual immorality; that each of you should learn to control his own body in a way that is *holy* and honorable, not in passionate lust like the heathen, who do not know God; and that in this matter no one should wrong or take advantage of a brother or sister. The Lord will punish all those who commit such sins, as we told you and warned you before. For God did not call us to be impure, but to live a *holy* life. Therefore, anyone who rejects this instruction does not reject a human being but God, the very God who gives you his Holy Spirit" (NIV).

In this particular passage, we are called to avoid sexual immorality and are three times called to be "holy."

The New Testament scholar Leon Morris writes these wise words:

> "The man who carries on an act of impurity is not simply breaking a human code, nor even sinning against the God who at some time in the past gave him the gift of the Spirit. He is sinning against the God who is present at that moment, against the One who continually gives the Spirit … This sin is seen in its true light only when it is seen as a preference for impurity rather than a Spirit who is holy."[157]

Let us recommit ourselves to a ministry anointed with power and godly purity. For we are entrusted with a high and holy privilege. By God's grace, may we finish well so that God's people will know that our ministry is worth their time, their trust and their treasure.

27.

RESPONDING TO TEMPTATION ON THE JOURNEY

Embedded in Genesis 39:8 are two wonderful words: "Joseph refused" (NET).

Joseph refused. Joseph resisted. Joseph rebuffed. Joseph ran. Nowhere do you find that when Mrs. Potiphar tempted Joseph with this seductive statement: "Have sex with me" (Genesis 39:7, NET), that Joseph reasoned with her. That was not a sheer subtle suggestion.

Verse 12 of that same segment of Scripture states simply that Joseph ran. What did Joseph call Mrs. Potiphar's temptation? "Such a great evil and sin against God" (Genesis 39:9, NET).

Joseph did not listen to her or linger in her presence (Genesis 39:10). Why? Because Joseph knows that lust is fierce, it is forceful, and it is formidable. Mrs. Potiphar says: "Joseph, you light up my life!" She even sings:

> It can't be wrong
> If it feels so right.[158]

"It has always been a mark of decaying civilizations to become obsessed with sex,"[159] writes evangelist Billy Graham. We encounter strong seductive forces that are alluring and attractive. That's why "before a king can rule others, he must prove that he can rule himself."[160]

Dietrich Bonhoeffer wisely writes that when the flame of lust is fanned, "God is quite unreal to us and … Satan does not fill us with hatred of God, but with forgetfulness of God."[161] Why? I'll tell you why. Because the accuser's desire is to destroy us.

Choosing sin to find satisfaction eventually leads to death. Paul Harvey writes this unforgettable parable:

> "I shall now recite the manner in which an Eskimo kills a wolf.
>
> "The Eskimo coats his knife blade with blood and allows it to freeze there. Then the Eskimo adds another layer of blood, and then another. As each succeeding smear of blood freezes to the blade of the knife, the Eskimo adds an additional coating until the blade is concealed by a substantial thickness of frozen blood. Then the knife handle is buried in the frozen ground with the blade up.

> "The marauding wolf follows his sensitive nose to the scent and tastes the fresh frozen blood … And licks it … More and more vigorously the wolf licks at the bait until the keen edge is bare. Feverishly now, he licks harder …
>
> "In the arctic night, so great becomes his craving for blood that he does not notice the razor-sharp sting of the naked blade on his own tongue. Nor does he recognize the instant at which his insatiable thirst is being satisfied by his own warm blood…
>
> "'More!' his carnivorous appetite craves, 'more!' Until dawn finds him dead in the snow."[162]

Ernest Hemingway tells us how Satan lures us into sin: "Gradually and then suddenly."[163]

One astute author describes our current culture with crystal clarity: "It is nearly as hard for a sinner to recognize the world's temptations as it is for a fish to discover impurities in the water."[164]

That's why when the New Testament lingers on the lure and lair of lurid lust, it gives us one clear command: "Run from anything that stimulates youthful lusts" (2 Timothy 2:22, NLT). In short, run from any satisfying stimulation. Richard Foster gets to the heart of the matter when he writes:

> "The demon in sex is lust. True sexuality leads to humanness, but lust leads to depersonalization. Lust captivates rather than emancipates."[165]

Being acutely aware of the snare of sexual sin and our propensity to spoil the good gift God has given us, the sincere and scholarly teacher from Tarsus tells us not to flirt with, but to:

> "Flee from sexual immorality. All other sins a person commits are outside the body, but whoever sins sexually sins against their own body. Do you not know that your bodies are temples of the Holy Spirit, who is in you, whom you have received from God? You are not your own; you were bought at a price. Therefore honor God with your bodies" (1 Corinthians 6:18-20, NIV).

What verses of victory! That's exactly what Joseph did. We too need to be acutely aware of the snare of sexual sin and our propensity to spoil the good gift God has given us.

Something else. "Resist him, firm in your faith," writes the former fisherman (1 Peter 5:9, ESV). Kenneth Wuest has a wise word of counsel here:

> "The Greek word translated 'resist' means 'to withstand, to be firm against someone else's onset' rather than 'to strive against that one'... Cowardice never wins against Satan, only courage."[166]

When you resist the devil through the power and in the name of the Lord Jesus Christ, the devil will back down. He'll back away. He will retreat as you resist him, firm in your faith. How do we form a shield to protect us from our adversary? (1 Peter 5:8, NASB).

> Take the name of Jesus ever
> As protection ev'rywhere.
> If temptations 'round you gather,
> Breathe that holy name in prayer.[167]

No one is immune to temptation. All of us are capable of falling. Paul, the once proud Pharisee admonishes us:

> "Therefore let the one who thinks he stands firm [immune to temptation, being overconfident and self-righteous], take care that he does not fall [into sin and condemnation]" 1 Corinthians 10:12, AMP).

Job offers wisdom for our day: "I made a covenant with my eyes not to look lustfully at a young woman" (Job 31:1, NIV). Job understands the wisdom of Proverbs: "Can a man scoop fire into his lap without his clothes being burned?" (Proverbs 6:27, NIV). Job's covenant forbids a second look. It means treating all women with dignity. This will incur their respect rather than their reproach. This is what sustained Joseph through the temptations of Potiphar's wife: "How then could I do such a wicked thing," he said, "and sin against God?" (Genesis 39:9, NIV), – and he fled.

The heart of the human problem is the problem of the human heart. The Russian writer, Aleksandr Solzhenitsyn, speaks of the unrestrained and unconverted heart: "The line dividing good and evil cuts through the heart of every human being."[168]

Solzhenitsyn was merely quoting Jesus who says with stunning sincerity and simplicity. Verbosity is not a substitute for veracity. The point is as simple as it is obvious:

> "Whatever comes from [the heart of] a man, that is what defiles and dishonors him. For from within, [that is] out of the hearts of men, come base and malevolent thoughts and schemes, acts of sexual immorality … adulteries … All these evil things [schemes and desires] come from within and defile and dishonor the man" (Mark 7:20-23, AMP).

Unlike the pious Pharisees of His day, Jesus' simple, straightforward style of communication is refreshing. That is why G. K. Chesterton remarks that this is the reason:

"Most critics who are offended at the things Jesus says are offended precisely because Jesus does not utter safe platitudes."[169]

28.

THE CONSEQUENCES OF SIN ALONG THE JOURNEY

Blaise Pascal painfully pens these honest words:

> "We have not sufficiently plumbed the wretchedness of man in general, nor our own in particular, when we are still surprised at the weakness and the corruption of man."[170]

We seldom fall suddenly into sin. Like erosion, the slippage is subtle, slow and silent. No married couple suddenly divorces. No home suddenly fractures. No church suddenly splits. Nobody suddenly makes one leap from the pinnacle of praise to the curb of carnality.

Our descent into sin is almost always gradual – the culmination of a lot of seemingly secret insignificant choices. C. S. Lewis observes:

> "The safest road to hell is the gradual one – the gentle slope, soft underfoot, without sudden turnings, without milestones, without signposts."[171]

It has been pointed out that:

- It was the breaking of the *Tenth* Commandment (coveting his neighbor's wife) that led David to commit adultery, thus breaking the *Seventh* Commandment.
- Then, in order to steal his neighbor's wife (thereby breaking the *Eighth* Commandment, he committed murder and broke the *Sixth* Commandment.
- He broke the *Ninth* Commandment by bearing false witness against his brother.
- This all brought dishonor to his parents and thus broke the *Fifth* Commandment.

In this way he broke all of the Ten Commandments that relate to loving one's neighbor as oneself (Commandments Five through Ten). And in so doing, he dishonored God as well, breaking, in effect, the first four Commandments.[172]

Cover-Up

In his relentless rage of lust, David deliberately compromised with wrong and deceitfully covered it up with murder. James, the brother of Jesus, writes with absolute accuracy:

> "But each one is tempted when he is dragged away, enticed, and baited [to commit sin] by his own [worldly] desire (lust, passion). Then when the illicit desire has conceived, it gives birth to sin; and when sin has run its course, it gives birth to death" (James 1:14-15, AMP).

The messenger came to the king from the battlefield. David waited and listened with bated breath for one significant statement: "And your servant Uriah the Hittite is also dead" (2 Samuel 11:24, AMP).

David finally fell. He tried to cover his tragic tracks. It was done secretly and surreptitiously. David's plot to have Uriah killed was done willfully. This was not a momentary mistake. He did not stumble into sin (2 Samuel 11:6-25). As Samson lusted in the lap of Delilah, David willfully walked into sin with Bathsheba, had her husband killed, and lived a lie during the months that followed.

I wonder what God has to say. God definitively declared: "The thing that David had done [with Bathsheba] was evil in the sight of the LORD" (2 Samuel 11:27, AMP).

For David as it is for us, "the pleasures of sin" make our hearts beat faster and they make us feel good. But one thing is certain, in the liberating letter of Galatians Paul carefully and clearly communicates:

> "Do not be deceived, God is not mocked [He will not allow Himself to be ridiculed, nor treated with contempt nor allow His precepts to be scornfully set aside]; for whatever a man sows, this and this only is what he will reap" (Galatians 6:7, AMP).

This is the transcendent truth. God gives us His Word to awaken an awareness that His moral and spiritual laws exist, and they govern our lives. Defy His laws at your own peril.

We tend to think that since judgment has not fallen immediately after we sinned, God must be okay with our sin. He winks at our sin and pretends it did not happen. The fact that God does not immediately punish our sin does not mean there are no consequences to pay. If we plant seeds of sin in our lives, we should not be surprised if we harvest a crop of sorrow, destruction, and death.

Sin has certain consequences, and forgiveness does not cancel the consequences of sin. God will forgive us, but we still have to deal with the broken marriage, the sexually transmitted disease, the lung cancer, the prison term, the humiliating loss of reputation that is the natural consequence of our sin.

These principles operated invariably and inevitably in David's life. But let's not deceive ourselves. They operate in our lives as well.

Confession

Listen to David as he writes months later in the aftermath of his sin:

> "How blessed is he whose transgression is forgiven, whose sin is covered! How blessed is the man to whom the LORD does not impute iniquity, and in whose spirit there is no deceit!" (Psalm 32:1-2, NASB).

Confession followed. The Living Bible records it in simple and stark terms:

> "There was a time when I wouldn't admit what a sinner I was. But my dishonesty made me miserable and filled my days with frustration. All day and all night your hand was heavy on me. My strength evaporated like water on a sunny day until I finally admitted all my sins to you and stopped trying to hide them" (Psalm 32:3-4).

We must confess our sins. C. S. Lewis writes with incisive insight: "We must lay before him what is in us, not what ought to be within us."[173] This done, we should confess each sin by its ugly name, and then thank God for His forgiveness through the blood of His Son.

The importance of confession cannot be overstated. "If I had cherished sin in my heart, the Lord would not have listened" (Psalm 66:18, NIV; cf. Proverbs 28:13).

The way to return to God is to acknowledge our sin. As long as our sin remains unacknowledged and unconfessed, we cannot return to God. We need to take sin as seriously as He does.

Confession not only opens the heavens, but it also enhances our intimacy with God. François Fénelon encourages us to:

> "Tell [God] all that is in your heart, as one unloads one's heart to a dear friend ... People who have no secrets from each other never want for subjects of conversation; they do not ... weigh their words, because there is nothing to be kept back. Neither do they seek for something to say; they talk out of the abundance of their heart – without consideration, just what they think ... Blessed are they who attain to such familiar, unreserved intercourse with God."[174]

Cleansing

With confession comes cleansing:

> "If we [freely] admit that we have sinned and confess our sins, He is faithful and just [true to His own nature and promises] and will forgive our sins and cleanse us continually from all unrighteousness [our wrongdoing, everything not in conformity with His will and purpose]" (1 John 1:9, AMP).

Even now, whenever the timeless truth of God's Word is proclaimed without compromise but with clarity, people are drawn to it. God's Word throws open the gates of the human heart so the Holy Spirit can come in – bringing conviction and cleansing.

Consequences

God dispatched prophet Nathan to confront David. Listen to the moving message of indictment from Nathan:

> "You are the man! Thus says the LORD, the God of Israel, 'I anointed you as king over Israel, and I spared you from the hand of Saul. I also gave you your master's house, and put your master's wives into your care and under your protection, and I gave you the house (royal dynasty) of Israel and of Judah; and if that had been too little, I would have given you more! Why have you despised the word of the LORD by doing evil in His sight? You have struck down Uriah the Hittite with the sword and have taken his wife to be your wife. You have killed him with the sword of the Ammonites. Now, therefore, the sword shall never depart from your house …' Thus says the LORD, 'Behold, I will stir up evil against you from your own household …'" (2 Samuel 12:7-11, AMP).

Someone once said that you can pull the nail out of the wall, but you can't pull out the nail hole. Rudyard Kipling put it in these picturesque words: "The sin they do two by two they must pay for one by one."[175]

In the days and years to come, David would experience grief within his own household. Nathan was prescient and prophetic. Turmoil and tragedy. Rape and revenge. An uncontrollable son. A son who betrays him, and who drives his own father from the throne.

Oh, the cascading catastrophic consequences of sin! They all begin with following through on sin's tempting thoughts. They then lead to a cycle of denial, deception, and spiritual destruction.

David's only realistic response to Nathan was: "I have sinned against the LORD" (2 Samuel 12:13, AMP). In Psalm 51, David specifically spells out his sin:

> "Against You, You only, have I sinned and done that which is evil in Your sight" (Psalm 51:4, AMP).

Concluding Thoughts

Every sin that is committed is perpetrated against God's "one and only Son" (John 3:16, NIV). That's why John the apostle who was exiled on the island of Patmos writes with pinpoint precision:

> "… the blood of Jesus His Son cleanses us from all sin [by erasing the stain of sin, keeping us cleansed from sin in all its forms and manifestations]" (1 John 1:7, AMP).

God wants to take our brokenness, the ugly stain of our sin, suffering and sorrow that appears to have ruined our lives and transform our brokenness into beauty. Or, as that prolific prophet-poet puts it, God gives us “beauty for ashes” (Isaiah 61:3, NKJV).

And my response can be found in the words of this hymn that I sang before the worship service for many years:

> King of my life, I crown Thee now,
> Thine shall the glory be.
> Lest I forget Thy thorn-crowned brow,
> Lead me to Calvary.[176]

29.

GOD'S FORGIVENESS ON THE JOURNEY

I have known numerous ups and downs, many failures yet many blessings from my forgiving Lord. I can safely conclude that I have seen more of the favor and forgiveness of God than I deserve.

Yet sometimes guilt slips in the unguarded gate of my memory and seeks to rob me of the peace that only Christ can give. Sometimes I rehearse past sin that had already been fully forgiven by God, but which had not been fully forgotten by me.

I do not know the pain of your past. In all likelihood, you had horrendous heartaches. A few memories you wish you could erase. Pain had invaded your life without invitation. Now they are like paintings that hang in the gallery of your mind, permanently etched in the creases of your brain.

I am blessed by Carol Owens when she writes these winsome words: "God forgave my sin in Jesus' name."[177] The greatest need of the human heart is to know that we have been forgiven.

What the perfumes of Arabia cannot do for the blood-stained hands of Lady Macbeth, the blood of Jesus Christ can do for our sin.[178]

That's why John the Beloved definitively declares: "The blood of Jesus His Son cleanses us from all sin [by erasing the stain of sin, keeping us cleansed from sin in all its forms and manifestations]" (1 John 1:7, AMP).

> What can wash away my sin?
> Nothing but the blood of Jesus;
> What can make me whole again?
> Nothing but the blood of Jesus.[179]

Have you been hearing the giant of unforgiveness lumber across the landscape of your life? I could not write this chapter without remembering the wise words of Amy Carmichael. With courageous confidence, I offer them for your careful consideration:

> "If I say, 'Yes, I forgive, but I cannot forget,' as though the God, who twice a day washes all the sands on all the shores of all the world, could not wash such memories from my mind, then I know nothing of Calvary love."[180]

It is a forgotten fact that you must at times confront, and at other times confess. The practice of forgiveness is essential.

30.
FAILURE ON THE JOURNEY

There is a dangerous and deceptive teaching that says that once you have failed, God cannot use you anymore. It drips with disappointment.

Allow me to turn the searchlight of Scripture on this false and fallacious notion.

What about Abraham? He was a liar. He uttered blatant lies on more than one occasion about his "princess" wife, with his wife's cooperation. Remember Sarah means "princess." But even after he lies, he came to be known as the "friend of God."

Is Jacob any better? He was a cheat who cheated his own twin brother out of his birthright. Yet even though he was a deceiver,

God lifted him up to new heights and gave him a new name: "Israel."

Do you remember Rahab? She was a prostitute. Yet God selected her as His special instrument to preserve the lives of two of His courageous servants. Her name is in the record in Hebrews 11 "Hall of Faith." Carefully consider that she is included in the ancestry and lineage of Jesus Christ.

David became known as "a man after [God's] own heart" (Acts 13:22, NASB), yet his life was soiled by a sordid sex scandal (see 2 Samuel 11).

What about the prodigal prophet Jonah? God used him to lead a spiritual awakening in Nineveh. An entire city repented. Remember, Jonah wanted destruction, but God gave deliverance.

You could not find two more dedicated men in the first century than Paul and Barnabas. Pastor G. Campbell Morgan agrees:

> "I am greatly comforted when I read this [disagreement between Paul and Barnabas]. I am thankful for the revelation of the humanity of these men. If I had never read that Paul and Barnabas had a contention, I should have been afraid. These men were not angels, they were men."[181]

Accompanying them was a young man named John Mark who was neither seasoned nor strong. John Mark left Paul in the middle of a missionary journey. But that was not the end of his work. He wrote the second gospel that bears his name. What did Paul say about him when Paul was in the Roman prison? Paul did not call Mark a deserter[182] or a defector.[183] Instead, Paul appreciates Mark's work and affirms it as significant:

> "Get Mark and bring him with you, because he is helpful to me in my ministry" (2 Timothy 4:11, NIV).

The New Testament scholar A. T. Robertson is right:

> "No one can rightly blame Barnabas for giving his cousin John Mark a second chance nor Paul for fearing to risk him again. One's judgment may go with Paul, but one's heart goes with Barnabas ... Paul and Barnabas parted in anger and both in sorrow. Paul owed more to Barnabas than to any other man. Barnabas was leaving the greatest spirit of the time and of all times."[184]

The history of the Church has a similar story as these broken saints in Scripture. They are living contradictions of saint and sinner. Yet, "the people involved … have loved God, followed Jesus, and received his Spirit."[185] John Calvin participated in burning a man at the stake. Martin Luther made racist remarks. George Whitefield owned slaves. John Wesley was an absentee husband.

I qualify for His service with all my faults and failures. And so do you. No matter what your past may have been, your future is brighter than you know.

Sometimes the faithful fail and fall. The path of the faithful is littered with the remains of those who once sang great "songs of loudest praise."[186] Baptist pastor Robert Robinson prophesies his own spiritual downward spiral:

> O to grace how great a debtor
> Daily I'm constrained to be!
> Let Thy goodness, like a fetter,
> Bind my wandering heart to Thee:
>
> Prone to wander, Lord, I feel it,
> Prone to leave the God I love.[187]

The good and the godly are flawed. I'm grateful and relieved to know that God's people do not have to be perfect to receive God's protection, His provision, and His promise to redeem us from our sin. No wonder we call it "amazing grace."[188] Pastor Alan Redpath provides us with a remarkable reminder:

> "The conversion of a soul is the miracle of a moment; the manufacture of a saint is the task of a lifetime."[189]

31.

RESTORED ON THE JOURNEY

Peter must have wondered, "Will my Lord ever forgive me for denying Him? How do I turn back to Him?" (Luke 22:32, AMP).

It was a misty Sunday morning, and the sky was dark. It was still and silent. Mary Magdalene and the other women visited the tomb darkened by the shadows of silent Saturday. The warm waves of sunshine have not broken through. The word to the women was: "Go tell His disciples and Peter" (Mark 16:7, AMP).

"And Peter!" The significance of those words cannot be overstated. Peter has been rescued by grace.

"My Lord still remembers me. Will He restore me?"

In one moment in time, Peter heard Jesus call his name. Aren't you glad that Jesus not only rescues you, but He also remembers you, and He will restore you? It is one thing to be rescued by Jesus, it is one thing to be remembered by Jesus, it is something else to be restored by Jesus.

Peter's Desire and Peter's Prayer

Listen to Peter's desire and Peter's prayer as it is sung by the incomparable Whitney Houston in 1988. The chorus encapsulates Peter's desire: "I want one moment in time" and Peter's prayer: "Give me one moment in time."

> I want one moment in time
> When I'm more than I thought I could be
> When all of my dreams are a heartbeat away
> And the answers are all up to me.
>
> Give me one moment in time
> When I'm racing with destiny
> Then in that one moment of time
> I will feel
> I will feel eternity.[190]

Peter's prayer was answered after the beach breakfast by the Sea of Galilee. There are only two places in the New Testament where the word "charcoal" is used. Once here:

> "When they got out on land, they saw a charcoal fire there, with fish lying on it, and bread" (John 21:9, RSV).

And here:

> "Now the servants and officers had made a charcoal fire, because it was cold, and they were standing and warming themselves; Peter also was with them, standing and warming himself" (John 18:8, RSV).

The same fire that warmed Peter at the beach now had also warmed him on the night of his denial.

Now, Jesus came to Peter in one moment in time and asked,

> "'Simon, son of John, do you love Me more than [others do – with total commitment and devotion]?'
>
> Peter said to Him, 'Yes, Lord; You know that I love You [with a deep, personal affection as for a friend].'
>
> Jesus said to him, 'Feed My lambs.'
>
> Again, Jesus said to him a second time, 'Simon, son of John, do you love Me [with total commitment and devotion]?'
>
> Peter said to Jesus, 'Yes, Lord; You know that I love You [with a deep, personal affection, as for a close friend].'
>
> Jesus said to him, 'Shepherd My sheep.'
>
> Jesus said to him the third time, 'Simon, son of John, do you love Me [with a deep, personal affection for Me, as for a close friend]?'
>
> And Peter said to Him, 'You know everything; You know that I love You [with a deep, personal affection, as for a close friend].'
>
> Jesus said to him, 'Feed My sheep'" (John 21:15-17, AMP).

Notice the contrast in the manner that Peter denied Jesus and the manner Jesus commissioned Peter. Peter denied Jesus three times ever so deliberately and decisively in the dark, but Jesus commissioned Peter three times ever so carefully and clearly during the day.

Peter became a changed man with a changed mission.

Bill and Gloria Gaither wrote these wonderful words in a song that Peter would certainly resonate with:

> Something beautiful, something good.
> All my confusion He understood.
> All I had to offer Him was brokenness and strife,
> But He made something beautiful of my life.[191]

Lewis Smedes states that:

> "A person who breaks a promise of loyalty violates a relationship based on promise and trust. We cannot go on as usual in the relationship unless the wrong of it is healed."[192]

Jesus did not commission Peter to humiliate Peter, but to heal His devoted disciple.

Do you fear that your flaws are too numerous, and your failures are too enormous for Jesus to give you a second chance to fulfill your destiny?

When God forgives, He forgets. He is pleased to use any vessel – if it is clean. "Create in me a clean heart, O God" (Psalm 51:10, RSV), prays Saul's successor, David. It may be cracked or chipped. But God's glorious grace says, "I want to use you again."

Jesus can use you. Indeed, He wants to use you like He used Peter on the Day of Pentecost.

In one moment in time, He is calling your name.

In one moment in time, He is restoring you.

32.

A JOURNEY OF REPENTANCE

Recently, many around the world were caught up in a "revival at Asbury, Kentucky." If ever we needed a revival, it is now.

In 1990, I wrote a dissertation on "Jonathan Edwards as a Pastor-Preacher (1703-1758)."[193] The First Great Awakening took place in 1734-35, and the Second Great Awakening took place in 1741-1742. In essence, God used Jonathan Edwards and others to bring about two major revivals in New England during his lifetime.

If revivals are important, I submit to you that repentance is even more important. Why? Because while a revival is a once-in-a-lifetime experience, repentance ought to be a daily experience.

Repentance

Repentance is vital to a right relationship with God. The Greek word for "repentance" is "metanoia." It means "a change of mind, regret, remorse." But biblical repentance goes beyond feeling sorrowful for one's sins. It calls for a return to the Lord through obedience.[194]

The message of repentance is specific and practical. It involves more than getting baptized and having a spiritual experience. It means changing one's life. In all of the categories of life – as a spouse, parent, roommate, employee, or boss – we are to practice our Christian beliefs, not just give mental assent to them.

If repentance is true, then it will influence and impact our giving, our attitudes, and our treatment of others. Repentance may begin with a sorrowful heart, but it must end with a decisive and deliberate action.

In a poll taken on spiritual life in America, the reliable George Gallup unearthed some remarkable results. A majority of Americans believe Christ rose from the dead and is a living Presence today, yet very few translate that belief into action. Gallup concludes:

> "There's little difference in ethical behavior between the church and the unchurched. There's as much pilferage and dishonesty among the churched as the unchurched. And I'm afraid that applies pretty much across the board: religion, per se, is not really life changing. People cite it as important, for instance, in overcoming depression – but it doesn't have primacy in determining behavior."[195]

What an indictment that "religion, *per se*, is not really life changing." Are there areas in your life that Christ has not changed? If so, what are they?

In *I Surrender,* Patrick Morley states that the church's problem is in the narcissistic notion "that we can add Christ to our lives, but not subtract sin. It is a change in belief without a change in behavior." He goes on to say, "it is revival without reformation, without repentance."[196]

Becoming an obedient disciple of Christ follows believing in Christ. Works follow faith. Behavior follows belief. The fruit comes after the tree is planted. Martin Luther reminds us:

> "No one can be good and do good unless God's grace first makes him good; and no one becomes good by works, but good works are done only by him who is good. Just so the fruits do not make the tree, but the tree bears the fruit ... Therefore all works, no matter how good they are and how pretty they look, are in vain if they do not flow from grace …"[197]

Paul, the eminent emissary of Christ, had a religious experience on the road to Damascus in which he encountered the living Christ. In that experience he "added" Christ to his life. But he did not stop there. His faith produced action. Notice what he said:

> "I proclaimed first to those in Damascus and Jerusalem, then to the whole region of Judea and to the Gentiles. My message was that they should change their hearts and lives and turn to God, and that they should demonstrate this change in their behavior" (Acts 26:20, CEB).

This is amazingly applicable to our lives today. God does not waste words. Notice the specific and strategic steps in that statement: “change our hearts and lives,” “turn to God,” and “demonstrate change in our behavior.”

In short, repentance allows the power of the Holy Spirit to flow freely in and through our lives.

Does our belief change our behavior?

33.

GOD'S FAITHFULNESS THROUGHOUT THE JOURNEY

Nothing in the Law of God or in the libraries of men is more realistic and relevant to you and me today than the faithfulness of God.

That's why the prophet Jeremiah writes: "His compassions fail not. They are new every morning; Great is Your faithfulness" (Lamentations 3:22-23, NKJV).

The Hebrew word Jeremiah used for *"faithfulness"* is the word "*aman,*" which means "so be it." It's the word from which we get our word "*amen.*" In essence, God is the *amen* to every one of His promises.

The ringing declaration of God's Word is this: "He who promised is faithful" (Hebrews 10:23, ESV). His promises cover every moment of our lives. They are as certain as His character. A devotional author writes:

> "He who has heard your prayers in the past will not refuse to supply your need in the present emergency."[198]

None of God's promises will ever fail, not even the slightest jot or tittle.

When I hear about the faithfulness of God, I immediately think of my own unfaithfulness. When we come face to face with God's faithfulness, we contrast ourselves because we keep messing up. But even here I have good news. The towering truth of God's Word says:

> "If we are faithless, He remains faithful; He cannot deny Himself" (2 Timothy 2:13, NASB).

That's why you and I can face tomorrow with eternal optimism because "Jesus is the same yesterday, today, and forever" (Hebrews 13:8, NKJV).

God's faithfulness falls like the dew on a misty morning. Jeremiah says: "This I recall to my mind, therefore I have hope" (Lamentations 3:22, NKJV).

We have to learn, even in the midst of life's most painful situations, to bring something to mind. We have to remind ourselves of God's unchanging faithfulness. We have to remember God's continual compassions, which are new every morning.

I love the hymn based on this passage, "Great is Thy Faithfulness."[199] The author, Thomas Chisolm, made one slight change. The hymn says: "Morning by morning new mercies I see."

But that's not what Jeremiah says. This is what Jeremiah writes:

> "Through the Lord's mercies we are not consumed, because His compassions fail not. They are new every morning; great is Your faithfulness" (Lamentations 3:22-23, NKJV).

Jeremiah did not see any visible morning mercies when He wrote Lamentations 3. He had no visible evidence of God's mercy at all. Morning by morning brought nothing but horror, pain and death. But Jeremiah said in effect, "Even if I don't see any tangible blessings right now, that does not alter God's mercy, God's compassion, or God's faithfulness."

That's why one of my greatest joys is singing:

> Great is Thy faithfulness, O God my Father,
> There is no shadow of turning with Thee;
> Thou changest not, Thy compassions, they fail not.
> As Thou hast been Thou forever wilt be.[200]

34.

NOTHING IS IMPOSSIBLE ON THE JOURNEY

In the afterglow of Queenstown Baptist Church's 60th Anniversary Service and Luncheon Celebration, I was convinced more than ever that I did not make a foolish and fanatical promise to serve God in full time ministry in 1971.

God took me back to the timeless truth of Scripture and repeatedly reminded me to walk confidently by faith rather than fearfully by sight (2 Corinthians 5:7). As I sat and worshipped God at QBC on November 26th, 2022, I told God that if He called me again, my answer would still be "YES!"

Serving God in full time ministry has been downright exhilarating and exciting. I am more enthusiastic in serving Christ now than ever. I agree with Bishop Handley Moule who says: “I’d rather tone down a fanatic than heat up a corpse.”[201]

“Nothing Is Impossible”

Eugene L. Clark was a gifted pianist and songwriter. However, he suffered from debilitating arthritis, which gradually affected every part of his body. Soon his eyesight was affected and he became totally blind. Before long, it became impossible for Eugene to continue playing the piano.

Unwilling to quit, he asked for a dictating machine to be brought to his bedside. He dictated his musical arrangements by the machine. Neither total blindness nor crippling arthritis could stop him.

His best-known song, “Nothing Is Impossible,” epitomizes his life. Written in 1966, I remember vividly learning this song at QBC.

> Nothing is impossible when you put your trust in God;
> Nothing is impossible when you’re trusting in His Word.
> Hearken to the voice of God to thee: “Is there anything too hard for Me?”
> Then put your trust in God alone and rest upon His Word;
> For everything, oh everything, yes, everything is possible with God.[202]

There are four passages in Scripture that address the subject of “impossibilities.” Two of them are in Jeremiah 32 and two are in the Gospel of Luke.

> "Ah, Sovereign LORD! You have made the heavens and the earth by Your great power and outstretched arm! Nothing is too hard for you" (Jeremiah 32:17, NIV).

Jeremiah reminds himself of the greatness of God. He recounts the history of Israel and he remembers how God had worked among His people. Then he concludes: "Nothing is too hard for you." What a profound statement to ponder!

Do you realize that whatever you call "impossible" is "nothing" to Him? Nothing!!!

"Nothing is too hard for you," Jeremiah said. God now turns Jeremiah's statement into a rhetorical question: "Is anything too hard for me?" (Jeremiah 32:27, NIV).

Like with aging Abraham and Sarah, God will see us through our barrenness. "At the appointed time I will return to you, at this time next year, and Sarah will have a son" (Genesis 18:14, NASB).

Sure enough, Abraham was one hundred and Sarah was ninety when Isaac was born. Their sarcastic snickering turned into a laughter of pleasure and praise. Isaac means "He laughs." "Is there anything too hard for the LORD?" (Genesis 18:14, NLT).

"Is anything too hard for me?" God is asking you to substitute your impossibilities with "anything." The bottom line is: "Nothing is too difficult for the LORD."

Next look at Luke 1:37. Connect those passages in Jeremiah with this message in Luke. It is an answer to Mary's question concerning her conception. An angel appeared to Mary and said: "You are going to bear the Christ-child."

Mary asks, “How can this be, since I am a virgin?” (Luke 1:34, NASB).

Do you recall the answer? “For nothing will be impossible with God” (Luke 1:37, NASB).

In Luke 18:27, our Lord Jesus said: “What is impossible with man is possible with God.” (NIV).

You have seen these four precious promises of God. Each has said virtually the same thing. “Nothing is impossible with God.” Is it your health? Is it your education? Is it your business? Is it your ministry? Is it your marriage? Is it your family?

Whatever your specific impossibility, God’s Word to you is: “Nothing is impossible with Me.”

35.

JOURNEY WITH THE RISEN CHRIST

As those who are created in the image of God, we are hardwired to long for more. This statement is attributed to Voltaire: "God created man in His own image, and man has been trying to return the favor ever since."[203] We have neither the authority nor the ability to change God into our image.

I also believe that hardwired into every fiber of our being ought to be the desire that Paul exquisitely expresses:

> "That I may know Him [experientially, becoming more thoroughly acquainted with Him, understanding the remarkable wonders of His Person more completely] and [in that same way experience] the power of His resurrection

> [which overflows and is active in believers]" (Philippians 3:10, AMP).

This is what Mark Pendergrass has in mind when he pens the lyrics of this moving song:

> The greatest thing in all my life is knowing You;
> The greatest thing in all my life is knowing You.
> I want to know You more, I want to know You more.
> The greatest thing in all my life is knowing You.[204]

If God's people will make knowing God and His Word the passionate pursuit of our lives, Satan will be thwarted in his every effort to divide, deceive, and destroy.

Through Jesus' death, burial, and resurrection, He defeated our greatest enemies: sin, Satan, and death. He overcame these enemies personally, powerfully and permanently. This is the essence of the gospel (1 Corinthians 15:3-4).

Trusting in the risen Christ is more than a mere intellectual exercise. Without the resurrection of Jesus Christ, there is no hope for us. Because of the resurrection of Jesus Christ, we're not fighting for victory, but we're fighting from victory.

Without the hope of heaven, there is nothing to prepare for, nothing to look forward to. Life becomes tedious and tiresome.

Christianity does not make much sense without the reality of heaven. Paul himself said that if we have hope only for this life, "we are to be pitied more than all men" (1 Corinthians 15:19, RSV).

God never promises to remove all our trials this side of heaven – quite the contrary! – but He does promise that there is meaning in each one. Our character is being perfected, our faith is being built, our "heavenly reward" is being increased.

Jesus portrays struggle for the Christian as a daily reality of our faith: "If anyone desires to come after Me, let him deny himself and take up his cross *daily*, and follow Me" (Luke 9:23, NKJV, emphasis added).

Gary and Betsy Ricucci's words have a ring of relevance:

> "Our Lord has sovereignly ordained that our refining process takes place as we go *through* difficulties, not around them. The Bible is filled with examples of those who overcame as they passed *through* the desert, the Red Sea, the fiery furnace and ultimately the cross. God doesn't protect Christians from their problems – he helps them walk victoriously *through* their problems."[205]

James Russell Lowell's famous words continue to ring true:

> "Truth forever on the scaffold,
> Wrong forever on the throne—
> Yet that scaffold sways the future,
> And behind the dim unknown,
> Standeth God within the shadow,
> Keeping watch above his own."[206]

Evidence of Jesus' Resurrection

Few historians deny the existence and death of Jesus Christ. The evidence for His resurrection is at once clear and compelling.

Charles Dickens' now famous line is apt and apropos when we consider the resurrection of Jesus Christ: "It was the best of times. It was the worst of times."[207]

One of the most interesting books I've read was written by English journalist Frank Morison, a skeptic of Christianity who wanted to disprove the resurrection. Morison poured over the evidence, hoping to demonstrate that it was a myth. But not only was he unable to disprove the resurrection, but the weight of the evidence also convinced him of the truth, and he became a Christian himself. His book, *Who Moved the Stone?* became a powerful defense of the resurrection.[208]

Luke, the historian, said that Jesus "presented Himself alive after His suffering by many infallible proofs" (Acts 1:3, KJV). For example, we are told that:

> "Jesus *Himself* stood among [His disciples] … they were startled and frightened … [Jesus] said to them, 'Why are you troubled, and why do *doubts* arise in your hearts?'" (Luke 24:36-38, NASB, emphasis added).

Here Jesus invites His disciples to doubt their doubts about His resurrection from the dead. Then He helps them by engaging their senses:

> "*See* My hands and My feet, that it is I Myself. *Touch* Me and *see*. For a spirit does not have flesh and bones as you *see* that I have. And when He had said this, He *showed* them His hands and His feet" (Luke 24:39-40, NASB, emphasis added).

Based on these encounters with Jesus, Peter would later write:

> "For we did not follow cleverly devised myths when we made known to you the power and coming of our Lord Jesus Christ, but we were *eyewitnesses* of His majesty [His grandeur, His authority, His sovereignty]" (2 Peter 1:16, AMP, emphasis added).

Similarly, John would say,

> "That which was from the beginning, which we have *heard*, which we have *seen* with our eyes, which we have *looked upon*, and our hands have *handled*, concerning the word of life – the life was manifested, and we have *seen*, and bear witness" (1 John 1:1-2, NKJV, emphasis added).

The twelve disciples were clearly convinced beyond any doubt of Jesus' resurrection that all but two of them (Judas and John) would later die as martyrs for the faith.

Simon Greenleaf, a founder of Harvard University School of Law, once an antagonist toward Christianity, came to believe in the historical, bodily resurrection of Jesus Christ. He wrote the book *Treatise on the Law of Evidence*, which continues to be esteemed by many legal scholars as the greatest volume ever written on the use of empirical evidence to prove or disprove claims concerning historical truth. Greenleaf concluded that any honest cross-examination of the evidence for the resurrection of Christ would result in "an undoubting conviction of their integrity, ability, and truth."[209]

Paul's Advice

Paul gives Timothy this word of advice that is amazingly applicable to us: "Remember Jesus Christ, raised from the dead, descended from David. This is my gospel" (2 Timothy 2:8, NIV).

Paul wants Timothy to remember that Jesus is risen and that He was raised from the dead by the awesome power of God. This same God was with Timothy in all of his trials, in spite of all opposition. He wants Timothy to remember that by God's power he could stand against the worst temptations and threats that might come against him.

As we journey with the risen Christ, F. B. Meyer, the English pastor, eloquently exclaims:

> "Oh, children of the Great King, let us pray that we may know the grandeur of our position before Him … heirs of God and joint-heirs with Christ! Called to sit with Christ in the Heavenlies! Risen, ascended, crowned in Him! Sitting with Christ, far above all principality and power! How can we go down – down to the world that rejected Him; down to the level of the first Adam, from which, at so great a cost, we have been raised …!"[210]

36.

GROWING IN FAITH ON THE JOURNEY

Growing in faith is a "daily choice"[211] and commitment. The late pastor Tim Keller says it best:

> "Believers understand many doctrinal truths in the mind, but those truths seldom make the journey down into the heart except through disappointment, failure and loss ... You don't really know Jesus is all you need until Jesus is all you have."[212]

What is Faith?

Faith is believing God is who He says He is, and that He will do what He says He will do. God wants us to walk by faith, not by sight (2 Corinthians 5:7, RSV). Martin Luther King Jr. expresses this need for trust:

> "Faith is taking the first step even when you don't see the whole staircase."[213]

Two of the most powerful verses in all of the Bible are found in Proverbs 3:5-6:

> "Trust in the LORD with all your heart and lean not on your own understanding; in all your ways acknowledge Him, and He shall direct your paths" (NKJV).

The hardest part for me on my faith journey is still the part of the verse that says: "lean not on your own understanding." I have a sneaking suspicion that it's the hardest part of your faith journey too.

Trust is not easy. It's much easier to walk by sight than it is to walk by faith (2 Corinthians 5:7).

We can only see the present and the past. The future is a little frightening to us. Elisabeth Elliott eloquently expresses:

> "Today is mine. Tomorrow is none of my business. If I peer anxiously into the fog of the future, I will strain my spiritual eyes so that I will not see clearly what is required of me now."[214]

So we need to hold on to His hand and trust Him to calm our fears. Rather, we need to let Him hold our hand on the journey.

Faith is Theological

If what God asks you to do always seems logical and makes sense to you, then you and I are living on different planets. I can resonate with what a fellow pastor experienced:

> "One of the most frustrating things about Jesus is that … He is constantly moving us away from the places where we would prefer to stay … And moving us closer to … where we do not want to go."[215]

This is why what Mark Batterson has written is helpful. He says:

> "Fath is not logical. But it's not illogical either. Faith is theological … It just adds God into the equation."[216]

Problems Grow Our Faith

None of us wants problems, but problems grow our faith.

Precious pearls are the product of pain. Had there been no irritating interruption, there could have been no pearl. Is it any wonder, then, that the gates of our heavenly home are made of pearls (Revelation 21:21). "As diamonds are made by pressure and pearls formed by irritation, so greatness is forged by adversity." [217] What encouragement that brings as the battle endures and exhausts us.

Problems also drive us closer to God. With tenderness, Hudson Taylor writes:

> "It doesn't matter how great the pressure is; what really matters is where the pressure lies. Whether it comes between you and God or it presses you nearer His heart."[218]

People Grow Our Faith

Sometimes God strengthens our faith through the word or presence of a community of believers. Dietrich Bonhoeffer says it succinctly:

> "Christians need other Christians who speak God's Word to them. They need them again and again when they become uncertain and disheartened … They need other Christians as bearers and proclaimers of the divine word of salvation."[219]

The story of Jesus healing a paralytic in Mark 2:1-12 is an excellent example of the power of community faith. Jesus was in Capernaum, teaching in a house. The crowd was overflowing the house. How would a paralyzed man ever reach Jesus in that crowd? He wouldn't on his own.

Fortunately, this man had four friends who believed Jesus would heal him. They put their faith into action by lowering their paralyzed friend through the roof into the room below where Jesus was teaching. Then comes the strong statement in verse 5: "When Jesus saw *their* [plural] faith …," He healed the man!

Perspective Grows Our Faith

When the disciples asked Jesus to increase their faith, He answered by telling them that if their faith was as small as a mustard seed, they would be able to uproot and cast a mulberry tree into the sea (Luke 17:5-6). In other words, the important issue was not the size of their faith; it was the size of their God.

Jesus' disciples needed the proper perspective to grow their faith. So do we. Ron Dunn reminds us that:

> "… faith itself has no power. It is not faith that moves mountains, it is God … Biblically speaking, faith, as a mere human activity, possesses no virtue, holds no merit, contains no power. The power of faith lies in its object."[220]

The writer of Hebrews tells us to "[fix] our eyes on Jesus, the author and perfecter of faith" (Hebrews 12:2, NASB). For our faith to grow, we must keep our focus on Him.

In *Disappointment with God*, Philip Yancey writes with captivating charm:

> "Only at the end of time, after we have attained God's kind of viewing, after every evil has been punished or forgiven, every illness healed, and the entire universe restored … Until then, we will not know, and can only trust in a God who does know.
>
> Not until history has run its course will we understand how 'all things work together for good.' Faith means believing in advance what will only make sense in reverse."[221]

It is hard to have your dreams dashed, to have your hopes unfulfilled, to face a future that is unknown and unfamiliar and unwanted. But God still has a way of guiding you to the destiny and purpose He has carved out for you.

37.

EXCELLENCE ON THE JOURNEY

One of the best-selling books in the late twentieth century was *In Search of Excellence*,[222] in which the authors highlighted companies that modeled standards of excellence in eight primary areas.

Our work must be done with an eye to excellence. Dorothy Sayers says that the Church in our time …

> "has forgotten that the secular vocation is sacred. Forgotten that a building must be good architecture before it can be a good church; that a painting must be well painted before it can be a good sacred picture; that work must be good work before it can call itself God's work."[223]

God's Commitment to Excellence

Genesis 1 records God's commitment to excellence when it says,

> "God saw everything that He had made, and behold, it was very good and He validated it completely" (Genesis 1:31, AMP).

Unlike the lukewarm Laodiceans (Revelation 3:14-18), Christians should always do good work. We ought to be the best workers wherever we are. We ought to have the best attitude, the best integrity, and be the best in dependability.

> "For we are His workmanship, created in Christ Jesus for good works, which God prepared beforehand so that we would walk in them" (Ephesians 2:10, AMP).

Being His workmanship, we are, as F. F. Bruce translates it, "his work of art, his masterpiece."[224] That's why Saint Augustine says it best: "A Christian should be an alleluia from head to foot."[225]

No Secular/Sacred Distinction

There is no secular/sacred distinction, for all honest work done for the Lord is sacred.

President John F. Kennedy visited the NASA Space Center in 1962. During his visit, he noticed a man who was carrying a broom. The president approached the man and asked, "Hi, I'm Jack Kennedy. What are you doing?"

"Well, Mr. President," the janitor answered, "I'm helping put a man on the moon."

The NASA janitor understood that he was not just pushing a broom. He was making history.[226]

Presbyterian preacher Frederick Buechner said that our work is a pivotal part of our calling:

> "The place God calls you to is the place where your deep gladness and the world's deep hunger meet."[227]

Luther's understanding of this revolutionized his life, and indeed the world of his day. He writes:

> "Your work is a very sacred matter. God delights in it, and through it He wants to bestow His blessings on you. This praise of work should be inscribed on all tools, on the foreheads and the faces that sweat from toiling."[228]

What we need is a work ethic that is informed by God's Word and religiously lived out in the workplace and the Church. The reason this is so important is that most of us spend eight to ten hours of our sixteen waking hours at work five or six days a week. So how we work not only reveals who we are but determines what we are.

To the Glory of God

Everything we do ought to be done to the glory of God. Listen to God's call to serve Him:

> "So whether you eat or drink or whatever you do, do it all for the glory of God" (1 Corinthians 10:31, NIV).
>
> "And whatever you do, whether in word or deed, do it all in the name of the Lord Jesus, giving thanks to God the Father through him" (Colossians 3:17, NIV).

> "Whatever you do, work at it with all your heart, as working for the Lord, not for human masters, since you know that you will receive an inheritance from the Lord as a reward. It is the Lord Christ you are serving" (Colossians 3:23-24, NIV).

Luther succinctly says: "Any and everything, if it is to be done well, demands the entire man, all his mind and faculties."[229]

Excellence is not just limited to my spiritual preparation; it includes making sure that my clothes are always pressed, and my shoes are always spit-shined. Why? I'll tell you why. Because the God I serve deserves my very best.

Like it or not, excellence does come with maturity. Of maturity, Fred Cook says succinctly: "It is the ability to do a job whether you are supervised or not; finish a job once it's started; carry money without spending it. And last, but not least, the ability to bear an injustice without wanting to get even."[230]

Worthier words have never been penned:

> Were the whole realm of nature mine,
> That were a present far too small;
> Love so amazing, so divine,
> Demands my soul, my life, my all.[231]

Enthusiasm

A parallel aspect of the Christian work ethic is enthusiasm. The word "enthusiasm" comes from two Greek words: "En" and "Theos." Put together, it means "to be filled with God."

I agree with the late Bishop Handley Moule who says, "I'd rather tone down a fanatic than heat up a corpse."[232] That's why Paul writes:

> "Whatever you do, work at it with all your heart, as working for the Lord, not for human masters" (Colossians 3:23, NIV).

The late Leonard Bernstein, composer and conductor of the world-renowned New York Philharmonic, was asked what he believed to be the most difficult instrument in the orchestra to play. He responded, "Second fiddle. I can get plenty of first fiddlers. But to get someone to play second fiddle with enthusiasm, that's a problem!"

Whatever you do, excellence is essential. I appreciate what Isaac D'Israeli wrote: "It is wretched … to be gratified with mediocrity when the excellent lies before us."[233]

This is my passionate and persuasive plea.

38.

GIVING THANKS ON THE JOURNEY[234]

Fifty-one years ago, I was young and dumb. Today, I am older and dumber.

My faith journey began at Queenstown Baptist Church (QBC) in 1966. It was at QBC that I received Jesus Christ as my personal Savior when I was twelve. It was at QBC that I preached my first sermon when I was fifteen. It was at QBC that I responded to God's call to fulltime ministry when I was seventeen. It was at QBC that I taught youths in Sunday school, led a Home Bible Study, and led singing, all in my early teens. It was at QBC that Rose and I started dating in December 1974.

I will never forget QBC leaders and youths who visited me when I was hospitalized for three weeks with a collapsed lung. Before I was discharged, the surgeon told me: "If you do not want your lungs to collapse again, you should not preach or sing again."

When I was released from the hospital, the first place I went to was the QBC sanctuary. This was what I prayed: "God, please allow me to preach the Gospel of Christ and to sing of the mercies of the Lord for as long as You give me breath."

Today, Rose and I have returned from America to tell you that God has answered that prayer.

Because you prayed for me, I was able to preach and sing for the last fifty-one years in Asia, in Israel, and in more than 750 churches across the United States.

Because of Daniel Soh's encouragement, I've written about my *Faith Journey.*[235]

I am committed to sharing my experiences gleaned from a lifetime of ministry with the next generation of courageous QBC young men and women who will be responding to God's clarion call to full time ministry. Because of Daniel's encouragement, Rose, my beautiful bride of 45 years, and I, have offered a small gift toward a Scholarship Fund at QBC today.

I first heard God's call to fulltime ministry at the Baptist Camp in Port Dickson, Malaysia in 1971. Daniel's investment of twenty dollars for me to attend the Camp has increased by over 1.5 million percent. For five nights, while over 200 young men and women from Malaysia and Singapore were at the campfire, I was in the dorm wrestling with God. Every night I could hear the melodious music coming from the crackling campfire.

Today on QBC's 60th Anniversary, God is calling the next generation of fearless men and women to full time ministry. If I can open the curtains of eternity, I can hear the angels singing:

> Jesus, Lamb of God, worthy is Your name.
> Jesus, Lamb of God, worthy is Your name.[236]

QBC angels, please stand to your feet, and join me in singing:

> Jesus, Lamb of God, worthy is Your name.
> Jesus, Lamb of God, worthy is Your name.[237]

39.
HOPE FOR THE JOURNEY

If this is the last time you have the privilege of delivering a story or song, let it be a message of hope.

Years ago, a submarine was rammed by a ship off the coast of Massachusetts and sank immediately. The entire crew was trapped inside. Every effort was made to rescue them, but they were unsuccessful. Finally, a diver placed his ear to the side of the vessel. Someone inside was tapping a message by Morse code. It was a question: "Is … there … any … hope?"[238]

Preaching must answer this vitally important question: "Is there any hope?" If you cannot offer people hope, then the message is not ready to be preached. The Bible profoundly portrays the jealousy of Saul, the loyalty of Jonathan, the courage of Nathan, the despair of Jeremiah, and the struggles of Paul. People deal with crippling emotions like guilt, doubt, futility, and fear.[239]

Examine the tapestry of life. Suffering is woven through the fabric of humanity. Many face the horrors of depression, discouragement, and disappointment. That is why, speaking to a group of young ministers three years before he died, Joseph Parker, a great preacher of yesteryear, is right: "There is a broken heart in every pew."[240]

With relentless regularity, people encounter hardship, heartaches, and headaches. No wonder John Eldredge says, "I don't trust a man who hasn't suffered."[241] Your task as God's messenger is to raise peoples' faces heavenward so that they can see beyond their circumstances to their celestial calling.

We can live several weeks without food, days without water, minutes without air, but we cannot live for one minute without hope. "To eat bread without hope is still slowly to starve to death."[242] Erik Erikson, a twentieth-century Danish American psychologist speaks these welcome words:

> "Hope is both the earliest and the most indispensable virtue inherent in the state of being alive. If life is to be sustained, hope must remain, even where confidence is wounded, trust impaired."[243]

Take away our hope and we are plunged into deepest darkness. No finer words have been written:

> "Take from a man his wealth, and you hinder him; take from him his purpose, and you slow him down. But take from man his hope, and you stop him. He can go on without wealth, and even without purpose, for a while. But he will not go on without hope."[244]

That's why the writer of Hebrews viewed hope as a source of stability: "This hope we have as an anchor of the soul, a hope both sure and steadfast and one which enters within the veil" (Hebrews 6:19, NASB).

That's why hope is not a philosophy; it is a Person. Therefore, "everyone who has this hope fixed on Him purifies himself, just as He is pure" (1 John 3:3, NASB).

Two Foundations

How does Jesus offer hope to His audience? Like rays of brilliant sunlight piercing charcoal-colored clouds after a storm, Jesus saved His best for His conclusion. With captivating charm, when our master-teacher reached the climactic conclusion of His message on the Mount (Matthew 5-7), He used a spellbinding story to clinch His point that left His listeners speechless, shaking their heads in amazement and astonishment.

> "Therefore everyone who hears these words of Mine and acts on them, may be compared to a wise man who built his house on the rock. And the rain fell, and the floods came, and the winds blew and slammed against that house; and yet it did not fall, for it had been founded on the rock. Everyone who hears these words of Mine and does not act on them, will be like a foolish man who built his house on the sand. The rain fell, and the floods came, and the winds blew and slammed against that house; and it fell—and great was its fall" (Matthew 7:24-27, NASB).

In this story that Jesus colorfully creates and constructs, one builder chooses to build on rock; the other on sand. The first builder hears and acts upon the truth. Interestingly, the second builder hears the very same things, but he stops there. He deliberately does not act upon what he hears. Jesus called the first builder "wise" and the second builder "foolish." It takes a storm to reveal which is which. It does not take a theologian to identify what the rock represents – Christ Himself. Simply stated, Jesus is the solid, stable, and secure foundation of our eternal edifice.

Life is like building a house. When you build a house, you can either build it on a firm foundation of the rock, or you can build it on sand. The rock is Christ – a loving lifelong relationship with Him. If you build your life on any philosophy, any purpose other than Jesus Himself, you are building your house on sand.

You can build a beautiful house on the rock, and you can build a beautiful house on sand. People driving by will admire that beautiful house regardless of what foundation it rests on. You might be able to live in your house on the sand for quite a while without experiencing any problems.

The reality is that "life is difficult,"[245] storms are inevitable, pain and discomfort do happen. Pastor Earl Palmer puts it this way:

> "We must prepare the houses we are building for wind, rain, and floods. We must prepare the child for the road, not the road for the child. There is a testing of all of the houses we are building, and that testing is built into the whole plan."[246]

The time of testing will come. James jolts us with these words:

> "Consider it all joy, my brethren, when you encounter various trials, knowing that the testing of your faith produces endurance" (James 1:2-3, NASB).

Notice that James, the half-brother of Jesus, does not say "if," but he gives us a definitive "when." Trials will buffet us as surely as wind follows winter.

The winds of adversity will blow, and the waves of trials will pound against the house. The testing you face may come from a troubling medical diagnosis, a devastating personal loss, a traffic accident that robs you of your health, a bankruptcy, the ruin of your reputation, or some other crisis. But I guarantee that sooner or later testing will come into your life. No matter how beautiful and comfortable your house may have been up until then, the time of testing will prove whether your house will endure. It all depends on your foundation.

The timeless truth of God's Word is not given to satisfy our curiosity, but it is given to change our lives. Spurgeon, the great Baptist preacher, expresses his convictions in these words of warning:

> "There are tens of thousands to whom the preaching of the gospel is as music in the ears of a corpse. They shut their ears and will not hear, though the testimony be concerning God's own Son, and life eternal, and the way to escape from everlasting wrath ... To what are these men like? They may fitly be compared to the man who built no house whatever and remained homeless by day and shelterless by night. When worldly trouble comes like a storm those persons who will not hear the words of Jesus have no consolation to cheer them; when sickness comes, they have no joy of heart to sustain them under its pains; and when death, that most terrible of storms, beats upon them they feel its full fury, but they cannot find a hiding place. They neglect the housing of their souls, and when the hurricane of almighty wrath shall break forth in the world to come, they will have no place of refuge."[247]

You may be experiencing the despair of the dank, dark dungeon where your dreams disappear and your hopes dissipate. You have been honest, you have done what was right, and yet a door has slammed shut in your face and now only doubts and fears reside.

You do not have to approach life with dread or despair because God can be trusted in tough and turbulent times. And He has not changed. He is still "able to do far more abundantly beyond all that we ask or think, according to the power that works within us" (Ephesians 3:20, NASB).

"The Solid Rock"[248]

Jesus' story prompted Edward Mote to write this song almost two centuries ago:

> My hope is built on nothing less
> Than Jesus' blood and righteousness;
> I dare not trust the sweetest frame,
> But wholly lean on Jesus' name.
>
> On Christ, the solid rock, I stand;
> All other ground is sinking sand,
> All other ground is sinking sand.[249]

In the midst of the struggles, the storms, and the sufferings of life, never doubt the presence of God. In the words of the late Francis Schaeffer, "He is there and He is not silent."[250]

This word of hope is as relevant today as when it was first recorded. The incredible importance of hope looms larger than life to me today. How powerful its presence!

For those who have trusted Christ, there is hope – whether we are basking in blessings or grinding through grief.

This word is for you. This word is for me.

40.
CELEBRATION OF THE JOURNEY

The late architect Frank Lloyd Wright recalled a day when he was nine years old, walking across a snow-covered field with his uncle. Wright's uncle was a practical man with an all-business attitude. As the boy and his uncle reached the far end of the snow-covered field, the uncle stopped and pointed backwards.

"Young man," the uncle said, "look at your tracks in the snow. See how they wander aimlessly from the fence to those cattle, to those trees, and back again? Now look at my tracks. See how they run straight as an arrow from there to here? I walked straight to my destination while you wasted time and footsteps wandering all around. There's an important lesson in this that I hope you'll always remember."

The boy did remember. Frank Lloyd Wright recalled that his uncle's words helped shape his philosophy of living – but not in the way the uncle expected. "I determined right then," Wright said, "not to miss most things in life as my uncle had."[251]

God never intended for us to only walk in straight lines. God intends that we should enjoy the journey. It is only as we enjoy the journey that we know how to celebrate the destination.

We have a future worth celebrating.[252] The Great Commission of our Lord Jesus Christ in Acts 1:8 will be fulfilled. How do I know? I'll tell you how. Because John writes:

> "After this I looked, and behold, a great multitude which no man could number, from every nation, from all tribes and peoples and tongues stand before the throne and before the Lamb … " (Revelation 7:9, RSV).

We live in the dash of Acts 1:8 and Revelation 7:9. We also live in the dash of our birth and our death.

A stonemason carved a headstone for a certain woman's husband with these traditional words:

"Rest in Peace."

A few months later, the wife discovered that her deceased husband had been unfaithful. So she returned to the same stonemason and asked him to add four more words. The stonemason did as he was told. Now the grave-stone reads:

"Rest in Peace …
Till We Meet Again."

When we meet Jesus, we have a future worth celebrating because "the gates of hell shall not prevail against it" (Matthew 16:18, ESV). Friends, you and I have a great future because when we place our faith in Jesus Christ, what He says to us is true:

> "In My Father's house are many mansions; if it were not so, I would have told you. I go to prepare a place for you. And if I go to prepare a place for you, I will come again and receive you to Myself; that where I am, there you may be also" (John 14:2-3, NKJV).

Victory In Jesus

One of the songs that Eugene Bartlett wrote is one of my favorite songs. It's called "Victory in Jesus."[253] Shortly after he wrote that song, he died.

Mrs. Bartlett became extremely sick because of the death of her husband. She lay in a comatose state in a Fort Smith, Arkansas hospital. For three weeks, she was not able to open her eyes nor speak a word. Somehow, the children thought that their mother wanted to see Eugene Jr. So they called for Eugene Jr. to come to their mother's bedside.

Eugene walked into the hospital room and came to his mother's bedside. Remember, this lady had not spoken a word nor raised an eyelid in three weeks. Eugene raised the oxygen tent, touched his mother on her wrist and said, "Momma, momma, this is Eugene Jr. Momma, is there something you want to tell me?" This mother, who had not spoken a word nor raised an eyelid in three weeks, opened her eyes to full measure, raised herself on her elbows, lifted her silver head from her pillow and began to sing:

I heard an old, old story, how a Savior came from glory,
How He gave His life on Calvary to save a wretch like me.
I heard about His groaning, of His precious blood's atoning.
Then I repented of my sins and won the victory.

O victory in Jesus, my Savior forever!
He sought me and bought me with His redeeming blood.[254]

Then she fell back on her pillow and went to claim the victory that was hers in Jesus Christ.

Days later, a friend said to Eugene Jr., "Isn't it a shame that your mother wasn't able to finish the song that your daddy wrote?" Eugene said, "Oh, she did. Momma and daddy made it a duet in glory."

Please listen to me. There's coming a great, grand and glorious hour when you and I will stand before Jesus in the throne room of heaven and Jesus will direct our attention to the millions there in heaven. "See, the millions who are here in heaven because you gave them the Word of God so that they came to know the God of the Word."

And there in heaven we will sing a duet in glory!

That's a future worth celebrating!

EPILOGUE
COME BEFORE THE JOURNEY ENDS

Few words in sacred Scripture are packed with pathos like these words in 2 Timothy:

> "Make every effort to come to me soon; … Make every effort to come before winter" (2 Timothy 4:9, 21, NASB).

Timothy was a young pastor of the church at Ephesus, located on the west coast of Turkey. Paul was in prison in Rome several hundred miles away.

Paul had hoped that Timothy would come to Rome and spend some time with him in prison – and that Timothy would do it before winter set in. In verse 13, Paul instructed Timothy to stop at Troas and pick up his books and stop at the house of Carpus and bring a cloak (an outer garment), which Paul had left there.

My dear sister and brother, the leaves of your life will turn to gold, red and yellow. They will be blown from the branches by autumn's winds of adversity.

Could this fall be your finale? T. S. Eliot exquisitely expresses it in this way:

> "All our knowledge brings us nearer to our ignorance,
> All our ignorance brings us nearer to death,
> But nearer to death no nearer to God."[255]

The more we know, the better we understand how little we know. Our knowledge brings us an awareness of our ignorance, and our ignorance leads not to life, but to death.

As Paul needed Timothy, you will need Jesus. The fragrant flowers of summer will soon be gone. The breathtaking beauty of autumn will soon be past. There's something strangely solitary about winter.

Paul was preparing for the bitter blast of winter. That's why he says to his protégé: "Come before winter."

Christ was the One who came to me before the many winters of my life. If you find yourself in a dark, damp, and distressing dungeon like Paul, you will discover that the One who came to you in the winter of your life is still the One who takes you by the hand.

Walk with Him day by day, and when the final day comes, you'll be ready to walk through the door of death, because you won't have to walk through it alone.

How refreshing and reassuring are the lyrics of this hymn! This is my prayer today and every day.

> Precious Lord, take my hand,
> Lead me on, let me stand,
> I am tired, I am weak, I am worn;
> Through the storm, through the night,
> Lead me on to the light:
> Take my hand, precious Lord,
> Lead me home.[256]

The living God, who revealed Himself in the Person of His Son, is the only Lord who, if you find Him, can truly fulfill you, and, if you fail Him, can truly forgive you.

Jesus is the only One who can guarantee you a home in heaven. He is the only One who can forgive your sins. He is the only One whose death paid the debt for your sins. Give Him your life now. By faith, accept His gift today. You'll be glad you did. Listen to the timeless truth of these lyrics.

> It is no secret what God can do,
> What He has done for others,
> He'll do for you.
> With arms wide open,
> He'll pardon you
> It is no secret what God can do.[257]

CONCLUSION

YOU ARE NOT ALONE ON THE JOURNEY

Socrates offers sage counsel in these wise words: "The life which is unexamined is not worth living."[258]

With pardonable pride, I consider myself blessed. Who am I that God should give me health and strength to be able to serve Him? Who am I that He has blessed me with a wife who has encouraged me enormously?

Having been in ministry for half a century brings some misty memories. However, the memories are as fresh as this morning's sunrise.

Nostalgia nuzzles its way into my heart. The immortal words from the Jewish musical are especially effective in describing my thoughts and feelings:

> Sunrise, sunset. Sunrise, sunset.
> Swiftly fly the years.
> One season following another,
> Laden with happiness and tears.[259]

Two Concluding Comments

I will leave you with two concluding comments. These practical principles are relevant for us today.

Giving Rather than Receiving

Firstly, Jesus Christ taught us the timeless truth that "it is more blessed to give than to receive" (Acts 20:35, ESV).

Peter Torjesen's heart was strikingly stirred by a challenge to missionary giving that he opened his wallet and poured all his money into the offering. The young Norwegian also included a piece of paper on which he wrote "*Og mit liv*" ("And my life").[260] This eighteen-year-old went on to serve faithfully as a missionary in China, until God called him home. He was only forty-seven years old.

Today, many buy things they do not need with money they do not have to impress people they do not like. There is absolutely nothing wrong with owning nice things, but something is terribly wrong when those nice things own us. Not so the Macedonian Christians.

> "In the midst of a very severe trial, their overflowing joy and their extreme poverty welled up in rich generosity" (2 Corinthians 8:2, NIV).

The Macedonians were facing a bleak and barren future. Even though they were economically strapped, they emptied their pockets and purses to help finance the spread of the gospel and relief to the poor through Paul. The Macedonians, who had fallen on hard times themselves, begged Paul for an opportunity to help provide relief for others who, like them, were suffering from economic scarcity. Their generosity was so profound and so public.

How did the Macedonian Christians give? "First they gave themselves to the Lord and to us [as His representative"] (2 Corinthians 8:5, AMP). First and foremost, we are to give ourselves to the Lord. When we do, our treasure will follow the leading of our heart. Truer words have never been spoken: "For where your treasure is, there your heart will be also" (Matthew 6:21, NIV).

God is not primarily concerned with our money, but with our motive.

We cannot outgive God. Our Savior offered us something we don't deserve and cannot earn.

Listen to the wise words from a trustworthy source:

> "You know the generous grace of our Lord Jesus Christ. Though he was rich, yet for your sakes he became poor, so that by his poverty he could make you rich" (2 Corinthians 8:9, NLT).

Jesus communicates clearly in these words:

> "No one can serve two masters; for either he will hate the one and love the other, or he will be devoted to the one and despise the other. You cannot serve God and mammon [money, possessions, fame, status, or whatever is valued more than the Lord"] (Matthew 6:24, AMP).

Pascal says that in each of us there is an "infinite abyss [that] can be filled only with an infinite and immutable object; … by God himself."[261] Therefore only God alone can provide the answer to the ache in our souls. C. S. Lewis writes: "God cannot give us a happiness and peace apart from Himself, because it is not there."[262]

George Bernard Shaw wryly writes: "The statistics on death are quite impressive. One out of one people dies."[263] When we die, we will not be able to take anything with us. A rich but wise man says:

> "Naked I came from my mother's womb, and naked I shall return there. The LORD gave and the LORD has taken away. Blessed be the name of the LORD" (Job 1:21, NASB).

Jesus tells us how He intends for us to invest our lives. He provides a prescription that is stunning in its simplicity yet foreboding in its difficulty. I want you to see how Jesus distils it in a single significant statement. Listen as He speaks:

"… first and most importantly seek (aim at, strive after) His kingdom and His righteousness, and all these things will be given to you also" (Matthew 6:33, AMP).

A preacher came to see a farmer and asked him,

"If you had $200, would you give $100 of it to the Lord?"

"I would."

"If you had two cows, would you give one of them to the Lord?"

"Sure."

"If you had two pigs, would you give one of them to the Lord?"

The farmer said, "Now that isn't fair! You know I have two pigs."[264]

Investing in the Next Generation of Leaders

Secondly, can you think of a more important investment than the next generation of ministry leaders?

The church today suffers from an alarming lack of leadership. Warren Bennis, the leadership guru, says:

"Leadership is a word on everyone's lips. The young attack it and the police seek it. Experts claim it and artists spurn it, while scholars want it … bureaucrats pretend they have it, politicians wish they did. Everybody agrees that there is less of it than there used to be."[265]

Moses was the greatest spiritual leader Israel ever had.

> "Since then, no prophet has risen in Israel like Moses, whom the LORD knew face to face, who did all those signs and wonders the LORD sent him to do in Egypt … For no one has ever shown the mighty power or performed the awesome deeds that Moses did in the sight of all Israel" (Deuteronomy 34:10-12, NIV).

But Moses was expendable!

> "And Moses the servant of the LORD died there in Moab … Moses was a hundred and twenty years old when he died …" (Deuteronomy 34:5,7, NIV).

I'm not getting any younger. Neither are you. Each new dawn and each golden sunset reinforces the repeated reminder that we are getting older. Because our journey on earth will be over one day, carefully consider the wise words of William James: "The greatest use of life is to spend it for something that will outlast it."[266]

The reason Christians all over the world invest their lives so sacrificially is simple: they have come to believe that God's gifts and graces are never meant to be hoarded, but always meant to be shared.

Why would David look at Mephibosheth, the orphaned son of Jonathan who was crippled in both feet, and offer reassurance that he (Mephibosheth) possessed the status of a royal son and that there would always be a seat for him at the king's table? (2 Samuel 9:13). I'll tell you why. Because David was compelled by mercy – not only as a recipient, but also as a generous giver of it.

The early Christians knew Jesus as the Prince of Peace who became poor, entered the world via a borrowed barn, had no place to lay His head, was in His appearance more homely than handsome (Isaiah 53:2), and left the world as a crucified common criminal.

That is why Rose and I are pleading the case and representing the cause of the next generation of ministry leaders in Singapore and the United States. I was the first one who responded to God's call to full time ministry from my home church in Singapore in 1971. With a special surge of gratitude, Rose and I have established a Scholarship Fund at Queenstown Baptist Church in Singapore for young men and women who respond to God's call to full-time ministry.

The Melody Still Lingers

The possibilities of praise are endless and exponential – a truth we will live out for all eternity. Matt Redman correctly concludes:

> And on that day when my strength is failing,
> The end draws near and my time has come;
> Still my soul sings Your praise unending,
> Ten thousand years and then forevermore.[267]

Long after Redman's song has ended, the melody still lingers.

A Lifelong Journey

Blessing the Lord is a lifelong journey; not a destination, even though God intends for us to enjoy the journey as well as the destination. That's why John Bunyan calls his classic allegory *Pilgrim's Progress*.[268] Because in that story, Christian traveled up and down on his seesawing journey.

We, too, are on a journey – growing and stretching. C. S. Lewis wisely writes:

> "Our Father refreshes us on the journey with some pleasant inns, but He will not encourage us to mistake them for home."[269]

Do not forget that this world is not our home; our true home is in heaven. One day our Lord Jesus Christ will welcome us with His "Well done" embrace. There is no greater reward.

My hope is that the preceding pages have sparked something in you that makes you want to bless the Lord on your journey. Because "the Lord inhabits the praises of His people" (Psalm 22:3, KJV), my prayer is that you will be "lost in wonder, love and praise"[270] along the journey.

You Are Not Alone

The good news is that you are not alone on your journey. Even when the whole world seems to be collapsing all around you, when there is no one you can depend on, no one you can turn to, you can rest in Him. The Lord will strengthen you and see you through anything. The Lord is your only source of strength in a time of trouble. Any other source will fail you. The hymn writer reminds us:

> When through the deep waters I call you to go,
> The rivers of sorrow shall not overflow;
> For I will be with you, your troubles to bless,
> And sanctify to you your deepest distress.[271]

I hope you will never forget what our living and loving Lord says:

> "And lo, I am with you always [remaining with you perpetually—regardless of circumstance, and on every occasion], even to the end of the age" (Matthew 28:20, AMP).

This is still God's promise to you today. His promise to you is sure and steadfast. His promise is to prepare you for the challenges and crises ahead. As long as the sun is in the sky, as long as the moon comes up at night, as long as the seasons change, God is with you.

In the midst of the struggles, the storms, and the sufferings of life, never doubt the presence of God. In the words of the late Francis Schaeffer, "He is there and He is not silent."[272]

You will ride through some dark valleys, but because He is with you, you will soar among the stars!

ENDNOTES

Chapter 1

[1] Scott Peck, *The Road Less Traveled: A New Psychology of Love, Traditional Values and Spiritual Growth* (New York, NY: Simon & Schuster, 1978).
[2] Patrick Pang, *Faith Journey* (Los Angeles, CA: Amazon, 2022).
[3] D. A. Carson, *The Sermon on the Mount: An Evangelical Exposition of Matthew 5-7* (Grand Rapids, MI: Baker Book House, 1978), 109.
[4] E. Stanley Jones, *A Song of Ascents* (Nashville, TN: Abingdon, 1979), 383.
[5] David McCullough, *Truman* (New York, NY: Simon and Schuster, 1992), 426.
[6] Terry Glaspey, *Pathway to the Heart of God* (Eugene, OR: Harvest House, 1998), 16.
[7] J. Oswald Sanders, *Spiritual Leadership* (Chicago, IL: Moody, 1967), 11, 12.
[8] John Henry Jowett, *The Preacher, His Life and Work: Yale Lectures* (New York, NY: George H. Doran Company, 1912), 114.
[9] "10,000 Reasons (Bless the Lord)," Matt Redman, 2011.
[10] Martin Luther, source unknown.
[11] Friedrich Nietzche, *Basic Writings of Nietzche* (New York, NY: Random House, 2000), 274.

[12] Charles Hadden Spurgeon, *The Treasury of David*, Vol. 1 (McLean, VA: Macdonald, n.d.), Preface.
[13] G. Campbell Morgan, *The Unfolding Message of the Bible* (Westwood, NJ: Fleming H. Revell Co., 1961), 232.
[14] "10,000 Reasons (Bless the Lord)," Matt Redman 2011.
[15] Eugene H. Peterson, *A Long Obedience in the Same Direction* (Downers Grove, IL: InterVarsity Press, 1980), 49.
[16] "Hallelujah Chorus," George Frederic Handel. Public Domain.
[17] Robert G. Rayburn, *O Come, Let Us Worship* (Grand Rapids, MI: Baker, 1984), 15.
[18] Richard J. Foster, *Celebration of Discipline* (New York, NY: Harper & Row, 1978), 106.
[19] Rayburn, *O Come, Let Us Worship,* 30.
[20] "10,000 Reasons (Bless the Lord)," Matt Redman 2011.
[21] Ibid., third stanza.
[22] Sissela Bok, *Lying* (New York, NY: Pantheon, 1978), 28.
[23] Charles Kemp, *The Preaching Pastor* (St. Louis, MO: Bethany, 1966), 26-27.

Chapter 2

[24] "There Shall Be Showers of Blessing," D. W. Whittle. Public Domain.
[25] "I Bless Your Name," Elizabeth Goodine, 2003.
[26] Warren Wiersbe, *Be Hopeful* (Wheaton, IL: SP Publications, Victor Books, 1982), 116.
[27] F. B. Meyer, *Joseph: Beloved – Hated – Exalted* (Fort Washington, PA: Christian Literature Crusade, n.d.), 24.
[28] "Just When I Need Him Most," William C. Poole. Public Domain.

Chapter 3

[29] John Ruskin, in *Quote/Unquote*, compiled by Lloyd Cory (Wheaton, IL: SP Publications, Victor Books, 1977), 158.
[30] François de Saligna de La Mothe Fénelon, *Christian Perfection* (Minneapolis, MN: Bethany House, 1975), 205.
[31] William Law, *A Serious Call to a Devout and Holy Life* (New York, NY: Paulist, 1978), 228.
[32] Fénelon, *Christian Perfection*, 90.
[33] J. Oswald Sanders, *Robust in Faith* (Chicago, IL: Moody Press, 1965), 175-176.
[34] Charles Bridges, *A Commentary on Proverbs* (Carlisle, PA: The Banner of Truth Trust, 1846), 41-42.
[35] Richard H. Bube, *To Every Man An Answer: A Textbook of Christian Doctrine* (Chicago, IL: Moody Press, 1955), 391.
[36] "To God Be The Glory (My Tribute)," Andraé Crouch, 1971.

Chapter 4

[37] Ernest Hemingway, *Farewell to Arms* (London, England: Vintage Classics, 1999).
[38] Leland Ryken, *The Liberated Imagination* (Portland, OR: Multnomah Press, 1989), 76.
[39] William Manchester, *The Last Lion: Winston Spencer Churchill; Visions of Glory: 1874-1932* (Boston, MA: Little, Brown and Company, 1983), 32, 33.

Chapter 5

[40] "He Knows My Name," Tommy Walker, 1996.
[41] "Because He Lives," Bill and Gloria Gaither, 1971.

Chapter 6

[42] "Come, Thou Fount of Every Blessing," Robert Robinson. Public Domain.

[43] "Lead Me to Calvary," Jennie Evelyn Hussey. Public Domain.

Chapter 7

[44] "Day by Day," Carolina Sandell. Public Domain.

Chapter 8

[45] Ray C. Stedman, *Talking to My Father: What Jesus Teaches About Prayer* (Portland, OR: Multnomah Press, 1975), 122.
[46] D. A. Carson, *The Sermon on the Mount: An Evangelical Exposition of Matthew 5-7*, 109.
[47] David M. Walker, *Comeback America: Turning the Country Around and Restoring Fiscal Responsibility* (New York, NY: Random House, 2009), 36-37.
[48] Rebecca Manley Pippert, *Out of the Saltshaker and into the World* (Downers Grove, IL: InterVarsity Press, 2021).
[49] N. T. Wright, *Early Christian Letters for Everyone: James, Peter, John and Judah* (London, England: Westminster John Knox Press, 2011), 10.
[50] Martyn Lloyd-Jones, *Studies in the Sermon on the Mount* (Grand Rapids, MI: Eerdmans, 1971), 28.
[51] Madeleine L'Engle, *Walking on Water: Reflections on Faith and Art* (New York, NY: Convergent, 2001), 113.
[52] John R. W. Stott, *Christian Counter-Culture: The Message of the Sermon on the Mount* (Downers Grove, IL: InterVarsity Press, 1978), 61.
[53] Jay E. Adams, *How to Overcome Evil: A Practical Exposition of Romans 12:14-21* (Phillipsburg, NJ: P&R Publishing, 1977), 47.
[54] Norman P. Grubb, *C. T. Studd: Cricketer and Pioneer* (Philadelphia, PA: Christian Literature Crusade, 1948), 166.
[55] Philip Yancey, *Soul Survivor* (New York, NY: Random House, 2001), 175.
[56] Fred Metcalf, *The Penguin Dictionary of Modern Humorous Quotations* (London, England: Penguin Books, 1987), 49.

[57] Marion Jacobsen, *Saints and Snobs* (Wheaton, IL: Tyndale House Publishers, 1972), 67.
[58] Dorothy Walworth, "General of the Army: Evangeline Booth," *Reader's Digest*, August 1947, 37.
[59] Merrill Tenney, *John: The Gospel of Belief* (Grand Rapids, MI: William B. Eerdmans Publishing Co., 1948), 215-216.
[60] "It Is Well with My Soul," second stanza. Horatio G. Spafford. Public Domain.
[61] Daniel T. Niles, *That They May Have Life* (New York, NY: Harper & Brothers, 1951), 96.
[62] John R. Rice, *Poems That Preach* (Wheaton, IL: Sword of the Lord Publishers, 1952), 68.
[63] Martyn Lloyd-Jones, *Studies in the Sermon on the Mount*, 2 Vols. (Grand Rapids, MI: William Eerdmans Publishing Co., 1959-1962), 2:219.
[64] Ibid.
[65] Warren W. Wiersbe, *The Integrity Crisis* (Nashville, TN: Thomas Nelson Publishers, 1988), 17.
[66] Brennan Manning, *The Ragamuffin Gospel* (Colorado Springs, CO: Multnomah Press, 2005), 11.
[67] William Shakespeare, *Julius Caesar*, Act 1, Scene 3.

Chapter 9

[68] Daniel Taylor, *The Healing Power of Stories* (New York, NY: Doubleday, 1996), 2.
[69] Theodore H. Epp, *Elijah: A Man of Like Nature* (Lincoln, NE: The Good News Broadcasting Association, Inc., 1965), 63.

Chapter 10

[70] F. B. Meyer, *Moses, the Servant of God* (Grand Rapids, MI: Zondervan Publishing House, 1953), 33-34.
[71] Ibid., 42.
[72] C. S. Lewis, *The Problem of Pain* (New York, NY: Collier Books, MacMillan, 1962), 93.

[73] Henrietta Mears, *What the Bible Is All About* (Ventura, CA: Gospel Light Publications, 1966), 33.
[74] "Draw Me Nearer," Fanny J. Crosby. Public Domain.
[75] J. Oswald Sanders, *Spiritual Leadership,* 108.
[76] "I Know Who Holds Tomorrow," third stanza. Ira F. Stanphill, 1950.
[77] C. T. Studd, source unknown.
[78] Amy Carmichael, "Make Me Thy Fuel," *Toward Jerusalem* (Fort Washington, PA: Christian Literature Crusade, 1961; London, England: Society for Promoting Christian Knowledge, 1950), 94.
[79] "I Have Decided to Follow Jesus," Simon K. Marak. Public Domain.

Chapter 11

[80] Source unknown.
[81] "I Serve a Risen Savior," A. H. Ackley, 1933.

Chapter 13

[82] Ben Patterson, *Waiting: Finding Hope When God Seems Silent* (Downers Grove, IL: InterVarsity Press, 1991), 102.
[83] V. Raymond Edman, *The Disciplines of Life* (Wheaton, IL: Scripture Press, 1948), 79.
[84] Reverend James Stalker, D.D., *The Life of St. Paul* (New York, NY: American Tract Society, n.d.), 67.

Chapter 14

[85] Warren Wiersbe, *On Being a Servant of God* (Grand Rapids, MI: Baker Books, 1993), 20.
[86] Patrick Pang, *Faith Journey.*
[87] Matthew Henry, *Commentary on the Whole Bible*, one volume edition, ed. Leslie F. Church (Grand Rapids, MI: Zondervan Publishing House, 1961), 408.
[88] Words from Jean Caudill to Rose and me in 1989.

[89] "I Know Who Holds Tomorrow," Ira F. Stanphill, 1950.
[90] Charles Bridges, *A Modern Study in the Book of Proverbs* (Fenton, MI: Mott Media, 1978), 3.
[91] Rosalind Russell and Chris Chase, *Life Is a Banquet* (New York, NY: Random House, 1977), 2.
[92] "When I Survey the Wondrous Cross," Isaac Watts. Public Domain.
[93] "I Know the Lord Will Make a Way for Me," Paul Epps, n.d.

Chapter 15

[94] A. W. Tozer, *The Root of the Righteous* (Harrisburg, PA: Christian Publications, 1955), 137.
[95] Dr. and Mrs. Hudson Taylor, *Hudson Taylor's Spiritual Secret* (London, England: China Inland Mission, 1955), 107.
[96] M. Craig Barnes, *When God Interrupts* (Downers Grove, IL: InterVarsity, 1996), 54.
[97] Warren Wiersbe, *Be Hopeful,* 116.
[98] "His Eye Is on the Sparrow," Civilla D. Martin. Public Domain.
[99] "Through It All," second stanza. Andraé Crouch, 1971.

Chapter 16

[100] "Higher Ground," Johnson Oatman, Jr. Public Domain.

Chapter 17

[101] Scott Peck, *The Road Less Traveled,* 16.
[102] Ross West, *How to be Happier in the Job You Sometimes Can't Stand* (Nashville, TN: Broadman Press, 1990), 54.

Chapter 18

[103] Joseph Bayly, *The View from a Hearse* (Elgin, IL: David C. Cook, 1973), 12.
[104] "The Lily of the Valley," first and third stanzas. Charles W. Fry. Public Domain.

[105] "Do You Know My Jesus," Vesphew Benton "Vep" Ellis, 1957.
[106] Ibid., chorus.

Chapter 19

[107] "I Know Who Holds Tomorrow," Ira Stanphill, 1950.
[108] Ibid., chorus.
[109] "Goodness of God," Brian Johnson, Edward Martin Cash, Jason Ingram, Jenn Johnson, 2018.
[110] Tony Snow, "Cancer's Unexpected Blessings," *Christianity Today* vol. 51, no. 7 (July 20, 2007):30-32.

Chapter 20

[111] Celeste Holms, *Reader's Digest Treasury of Modern Quotations* (New York, NY: Reader's Digest Press), 484.
[112] Christopher Morley, source unknown.
[113] Ralph Waldo Emerson, *Familiar Quotations*, ed., John Bartlett (Boston, MA: Little, Brown and Company, 1955). 502.
[114] A. T. Robertson, "The Acts of the Apostles," *Word Pictures in the New Testament*, Vol. 3, 241.
[115] Samuel Johnson, in Bartlett, *Familiar Quotations*, 355.
[116] Dan Allender and Tremper Longman III, *Intimate Allies* (Wheaton, IL: Tyndale House, 1995), 101.

Chapter 21

[117] W. Philip Keller, *Rabboni* (Old Tappan, NJ: Fleming H. Revell Co., Power Books, 1977), 78-79.
[118] "Trust and Obey," John H. Sammis. Public Domain.

Chapter 22

[119] Phyllis Thompson, *D. E. Hoste* (London, England: China Inland Mission, n.d.), 122.

[120] G. K. Chesterton, in Bartlett, *Familiar Quotations*, 742.
[121] Winston Churchill, in Bartlett, *Familiar Quotations*, 621.
[122] J. Oswald Sanders, *Robust in Faith*, 181.
[123] Elisabeth Elliott, *Shadows of the Almighty: The Life and Testament of Jim Elliott* (New York, NY: Harper and Brothers, Publishers, 1958), 15.
[124] John Pollock, *Moody* (Chicago, IL: Moody Press, 1983), 51.
[125] Patrick Pang, *Faith Journey*, 46-49.
[126] Ann Wells, "What Are You Waiting For?" *Los Angeles Times*, 14 April 1985.

Chapter 23

[127] "You're Nobody Till Somebody Loves You," Russ Morgan, Larry Stock, James Cavanaugh, 1944.
[128] Derek Kidner, *Genesis: An Introduction and Commentary* (Downers Grove, IL: InterVarsity Press, 1967), 160.
[129] "The Love of God is Greater Far," third stanza. Frederick M. Lehman. Public Domain.
[130] David Jeremiah, *God Loves You—He Always Has, He Always Will* (New York, NY: Faith Works, 2012), 119-120.
[131] C. S. Lewis, *The Problem of Pain*, 81.
[132] William Bell Riley, *The Perennial Revival: A Plea for Evangelism* (Philadelphia, PA: American Baptist Publication Society, 1916), 37-38.
[133] "A New Commandment," Roy Crabtree, 1973.
[134] William Law, *A Serious Call to a Devout and Holy Life,* 294.
[135] Katherine Anne Porter, "The Necessary Enemy," *The Collected Essays and Occasional Writings of Katherine Anne Porter* (New York, NY: Delacorte, 1970), 184.
[136] Alexander Whyte, *Old Testament Characters* (Grand Rapids, MI: Kregal Publications, 1990), 379.

Chapter 24

[137] Charles Colson, *Loving God* (Grand Rapids, MI: Zondervan, 1996), 92.
[138] Martyn Lloyd-Jones, *Romans: The New Man, An Exposition of Chapter 6* (Grand Rapids, MI: Zondervan Publishing House, 1973), 8-9.
[139] Dietrich Bonhoeffer, *The Cost of Discipleship* (New York, NY: Simon & Schuster, 1995), 44-45.
[140] Archibald Robertson and Alfred Plummer, *The International Critical Commentary, A Critical and Exegetical Commentary on the First Epistle of Paul to the Corinthians* (Edinburgh, Scotland: T. & T. Clark, 1961), 141.
[141] "Rock of Ages," third stanza. Augustus Toplady. Public Domain.
[142] A. W. Tozer, *The Root of the Righteous*, 137.
[143] "Amazing Grace," John Newton, 1772.
[144] "Amazing Grace (My Chains Are Gone)," Chris Tomlin, 2011.
[145] "And Can It Be," fourth stanza. Charles Wesley. Public Domain.
[146] John Blanchard, *Truth for Life* (West Sussex, England: H.E. Walter Ltd., 1982), 239.
[147] Greenville MacDonald, *George MacDonald and His Wife* (a reprint of a 1924 ed.) (New York, NY: Johnson Reproductions, a subdivision of Harcourt, Brace Jovanovich, n.d.), 172.

Chapter 25

[148] Donald Grey Barnhouse, *Romans, Man's Ruin,* Vol. 1 (Grand Rapids, MI: William B. Eerdmans Publishing Company, 1952), 72.
[149] William Shakespeare, *The Merchant of Venice*, IV. 1.
[150] "Day by Day," Carolina Sandell. Public Domain.
[151] "At Calvary," William H. Newell. Public Domain.

Chapter 26

[152] J. Oswald Sanders, *Robust in Faith*, 121.
[153] Dietrich Bonhoeffer, *Temptation* (New York, NY: Macmillan, 1953), 116-117.
[154] Ibid.
[155] J. Allan Peterson, *The Myth of the Greener Grass* (Wheaton, IL: Tyndale House, 1983), 29.
[156] F. B. Meyer, *David: Shepherd, Psalmist, King* (Fort Washington, PA: Christian Literature Crusade, 1977), 195.
[157] Leon Morris, *The First and Second Epistles to the Thessalonians* (Grand Rapids, MI: Eerdmans, 1959), 128.

Chapter 27

[158] "You Light Up My Life," Joe Brooks, 1977.
[159] Billy Graham, *World Aflame* (New York, NY: Doubleday, 1965), 20.
[160] Warren Wiersbe, *Wiersbe's Expository Outlines on the New Testament* (Wheaton, IL: Victor, 1992), 21.
[161] Dietrich Bonhoeffer, *Temptation,* 116-117.
[162] Paul Harvey, "The Eskimo and the Wolf," *The Florence Times*, August 21, 1966.
[163] Ernest Hemingway, *The Sun Also Rises* (New York, NY: Charles Scribner's Sons, 1926), 136.
[164] Eugene H. Peterson, *A Long Obedience in the Same Direction,* 15.
[165] Richard J. Foster, *Money, Sex and Power: The Challenge of the Disciplined Life* (San Francisco, CA: Harper & Row, 1985), 13.
[166] Kenneth S. Wuest, *First Peter: In the Greek New Testament* (Grand Rapids, MI: Eerdmans, 1956), 130.
[167] "Take the Name of Jesus with You," Lydia Baxter. Public Domain.

[168] Aleksandr Solzhenitsyn, *The Gulag Archipelago, 1918-1986: An Experiment in Literary Investigation,* Vol. 1 (Boulder, CO: Westview Press, 1998), 168.
[169] G. K. Chesterton, *The Everlasting Man* (New York, NY: Doubleday, 1974), 194-95.

Chapter 28

[170] Blaise Pascal, *Pensées* (New York, NY: Penguin Books, 1966), 75.
[171] Randy Alcorn, *Heaven* (Wheaton, IL: Tyndale, 2004), 23.
[172] J. Oswald Sanders, *Bible Men of Faith* (Chicago, IL: Moody Press, 1974), 13.
[173] C. S. Lewis, *Letters to Malcolm: Chiefly on Prayer* (New York, NY: Harcourt, Brace & World, 1964), 22.
[174] George Arthur Buttrick, ed., *The Interpreter's Bible*, Vol. 8 (New York, NY: Abingdon Press, 1952), 725.
[175] Rudyard Kipling, "Tomlinson," *Collected Verse of Rudyard Kipling* (Garden City, NY: Doubleday, 1916), 241.
[176] "Lead Me to Calvary," Jenny Evelyn Hussey. Public Domain.

Chapter 29

[177] "Freely, Freely," Carol Owens, 1972.
[178] William Shakespeare, *Macbeth*, V. 1. 2.
[179] "Nothing But The Blood Of Jesus," Robert Lowry. Public Domain.
[180] Amy Carmichael, *If* (Montreal, Canada: Christian Literature Crusade, n.d.), 48.

Chapter 30

[181] G. Campbell Morgan, *Acts of the Apostles* (Old Tappan, NJ: Fleming H. Revell, 1924), 369.
[182] William Barclay, *The Acts of the Apostles* (Edinburgh, Scotland: The Saint Andrews Press, 1964), 107.

[183] Ibid., 108.
[184] A. T. Robertson, "The Acts of the Apostles," *Word Pictures in the New Testament*, Vol. 3, 241.
[185] Andrew Wilson, "The Strange Encouragement of the Church's Appalling History," *Christianity Today*, March 17, 2017.
[186] "Come, Thou Fount of Every Blessing," first stanza. Robert Robinson. Public Domain.
[187] Ibid., third stanza.
[188] "Amazing Grace," John Newton and Chris Tomlin, 1772, 2011.
[189] Alan Redpath, *The Making of a Man of God: Lessons from the Life of David* (Grand Rapids, MI: Revell Co., 2004), 9.

Chapter 31

[190] "One Moment in Time," Albert Hammond and John Bettis, 1988.
[191] "Something Beautiful," Bill and Gloria Gaither, 1971.
[192] Lewis B. Smedes, *Forgive & Forget: Healing the Hurts We Don't Deserve* (New York, NY: Simon & Schuster, 1984), 33-34.

Chapter 32

[193] Patrick Pang, *A Study of Jonathan Edwards as a Pastor-Preacher*, D. Min. Dissertation (Pasadena, CA: Fuller Theological Seminary, 1990).
[194] C. E. B. Cranfield, *The Gospel According to Saint Mark,* rev. ed. (London, England: Cambridge University Press, 1972), 44-45.
[195] George H. Gallup, "Vital Signs," *Leadership*, Fall 1987, 17.
[196] Patrick M. Morley, *I Surrender: Submitting to Christ in the Details of Life* (Brentwood, TN: Wohlgemuth and Hyatt, Publishers, 1990), 14.
[197] Martin Luther, *What Luther Says,* Vol. 2 (St. Louis, MO: Concordia Publishing House, 1959), 614.

Chapter 33

[198] A. W. Pink, *The Attributes of God* (Grand Rapids, MI: Baker Book House, 1975), 92.
[199] "Great Is Thy Faithfulness," Thomas Chisholm. Public Domain.
[200] Ibid., first stanza.

Chapter 34

[201] David Wiersbe and Warren W. Wiersbe, *Making Sense of the Ministry* (Grand Rapids, MI: Baker Book House, 1983), 43.
[202] "Nothing Is Impossible," Eugene L. Clark, 1966.

Chapter 35

[203] Voltaire, source unknown.
[204] "The Greatest Thing," first stanza. Mark D. Pendergrass, 1977.
[205] Gary and Betsy Ricucci, *Love That Lasts: Making a Magnificent Marriage* (Gaithersburg, MD: PDI Communications, 1993), 50.
[206] James Russell Lowell, in Bartlett, *Familiar Quotations*, 567.
[207] Charles Dickens, *A Tale of Two Cities* (London, England: Chapman and Hall, 1859, Book 1, Chapter 1).
[208] Frank Morison, *Who Moved the Stone?* (Grand Rapids, MI: Zondervan, 1987).
[209] Simon Greenleaf, *An Examination of the Testimony of the Four Evangelists by the Rules Administered in Courts of Justice* (Boston, MA: Charles C. Little and James Brown, 1846), 37.
[210] F. B. Meyer, *Our Daily Homily*, Homily 183, Nehemiah 6:3 Christian Classics Ethereal Library.

Chapter 36

[211] Ben Patterson, *Waiting: Finding Hope When God Seems Silent,* 101-102.

[212] Tim Keller, *Walking with God Through Pain and Suffering* (New York, NY: Penguin Group, 2013), 5.
[213] "MLK Quote of the Week: Faith Is Taking the First Step ..." *The King Center*, February 21, 2013.
[214] Elisabeth Elliott, *Keep A Quiet Heart* (Ann Arbor, MI: Vine Books, 1995), 84.
[215] M. Craig Barnes, When God Interrupts, 54.
[216] Mark Batterson, *Wild Goose Chase: Reclaim the Adventure of Pursuing God* (Colorado Springs, CO: Multnomah Books, 2008), 79.
[217] Peter Gibbon, *A Call to Heroism* (New York, NY: Atlantic Monthly Press, 2002), 182.
[218] Dr. and Mrs. Hudson Taylor, *Hudson Taylor's Spiritual Secret* (London, England: China Inland Mission, 1955), 107.
[219] Dietrich Bonhoeffer, *Life Together* (Minneapolis, MN: Fortress Press, 2005), 32.
[220] Ron Dunn, *Faith Crisis: What Faith Isn't and Why It Doesn't Always Do What You Want* (Colorado Springs, CO: Life Journey, 2007), 35.
[221] Philip Yancey, *Disappointment with God: Three Questions No One Asks Aloud* (Grand Rapids, MI: Zondervan, 1988), 200-201.

Chapter 37

[222] Thomas J. Peters and Robert H. Waterman, *In Search of Excellence* (New York, NY: Harper & Row, 1982).
[223] Dorothy Sayers, *Creed of Chaos* (New York, NY: Harcourt, Brace and Company, 1949), 57.
[224] F. F. Bruce, *The Epistle to the Ephesians* (London, England: Pickering & Inglis, 1973), 52.
[225] Eugene H. Peterson, *A Long Obedience in the Same Direction*, 49.
[226] "What a NASA Janitor Can Teach Us About Living a Bigger Life," 9News.com. December 24, 2014.
[227] Frederick Buechner, *Wishful Thinking: A Theological ABC* (New York, NY: Harper & Row, 1973), 93.

[228] Ewald M. Plass, *What Luther Says,* Vol. 3 (Saint Louis, MO: Concordia, 1959), 1493.
[229] H. G. Haile, *Luther: An Experiment in Biography* (Garden City, NY: Doubleday, 1980), 56.
[230] Fred Cook, in Cory, *Quote/Unquote*, 200.
[231] "When I Survey the Wondrous Cross," fourth stanza. Isaac Watts. Public Domain.
[232] David Wiersbe and Warren W. Wiersbe, *Making Sense of the Ministry*, 43.
[233] Isaac D'Israeli, in Bartlett, *Familiar Quotations*, 417.

Chapter 38

[234] This three-minute speech was delivered during Queenstown Baptist Church's 60th Anniversary Luncheon Celebration on November 27th, 2022, at Roland Restaurant, Singapore.
[235] Patrick Pang, *Faith Journey.*
[236] "You Are My All in All," Dennis Jernigan, 1990.
[237] Ibid.

Chapter 39

[238] Ben Patterson, *The Grand Essentials* (Waco, TX: Word Books, 1987), 35.
[239] Charles Kemp, *The Preaching Pastor*, 26-27.
[240] Mac Brunson, "The Healing Power of the Word," https://preachingsource.com – blog, January 13, 2020.
[241] John Eldredge, *Young at Heart* (Nashville, TN: Thomas Nelson Publishers, 2001), 137.
[242] Pearl S. Buck, source unknown.
[243] Erik Erikson, source unknown.
[244] C. Neil Strait, in Cory, *Quote/Unquote*, 156.
[245] Scott Peck, *The Road Less Traveled*, 1.
[246] Earl F. Palmer, *The Enormous Exception* (Waco, TX: Word Books, 1986), 143.

[247] Charles Haddon Spurgeon, "On Laying Foundations," in Vol. 29 of *Metropolitan Tabernacle Pulpit* (London, England: Banner of Truth, 1971), 49-50.
[248] "The Solid Rock," Edward Mote. Public Domain.
[249] Ibid., first stanza.
[250] Francis Schaeffer, *He Is There, and He Is Not Silent* (Wheaton, IL: Tyndale House Publishers, 1972).

Chapter 40

[251] Mark Buchanan, *Your God Is Too Safe: Rediscovering the Wonder of a God You Can't Control* (Colorado Springs, CO: WaterBrook Multnomah, 2001), 102.
[252] I preached my first sermon in 1969 at Queenstown Baptist Church, Singapore. This is a brief excerpt of the message I preached at the First Institutional Baptist Church in Phoenix, Arizona in November 2019 on the occasion of the fiftieth year of my preaching ministry. FIBC is pastored by my good friend and brother, the Rev. Dr. Warren H. Stewart Sr. for the last 47 years!
[253] "Victory in Jesus," Eugene M. Bartlett, 1939.
[254] Ibid., first stanza.

Epilogue

[255] T. S. Eliot, *The Rock: A Pageant Play* (New York, NY: Harcourt, Brace and Co., 1934), 7.
[256] "Precious Lord, Take My Hand," Thomas A. Dorsey. Public Domain.
[257] "It Is No Secret," Stuart Hamblen, 1950.

Conclusion

[258] Socrates, in Bartlett, *Familiar Quotations*, 20.
[259] "Sunrise, Sunset," in *Fiddler on the Roof.* Jerry Bock and Sheldon Harnick, 1971.
[260] Kari Torjesen Malcolm, *We Signed Away Our Lives* (Downers Grove, IL: InterVarsity Press, 1990), 23.

[261] Blaise Pascal, *Pensées*, 75.
[262] C. S. Lewis, *Mere Christianity* (New York, NY: HarperOne, 1980), 50.
[263] Billy Graham, *Death and Life After* (Nashville, TN: Thomas Nelson Publishers, 2011), 3.
[264] John F. MacArthur, Jr., *Giving: God's Way* (Wheaton, IL: Tyndale House, 1979), 92.
[265] Warren Bennis & Burt Nanus, *Leaders: The Strategies for Taking Charge* (New York, NY: Harper & Row, 1985), 1.
[266] William James, in Cory, *Quote/Unquote*, 181.
[267] "10,000 Reasons (Bless the Lord)," Matt Redman 2011.
[268] John Bunyan, *Pilgrim's Progress* (New York, NY: Barnes and Noble, 2005).
[269] C. S. Lewis, *The Problem of Pain*, in *The Complete C. S. Lewis Signature Classics* (New York, NY: HarperOne, 2002), 618.
[270] "Love Divine, All Love Excelling," fourth stanza. Charles Wesley. Public Domain.
[271] "How Firm a Foundation," third stanza. George Keith. Public Domain.
[272] Francis Schaeffer, *He Is There, and He Is Not Silent.*

ABOUT THE AUTHOR

Dr. Patrick Pang is the Executive Director of Great Commission International Partnerships (GCIP). The mission of GCIP is to raise up the next generation of ministry leaders to be world changers in ministry and mission globally. Bible translation for people without God's Word in Indonesia is one of many wonderful ways that this takes shape.

Previously, Patrick served as the Senior Vice President for Advancement and Church Relations with Rainbow Acres.

An adjunct faculty member at Union University in Jackson, TN, Patrick has taught seminary courses in Preaching, Missions, and Stewardship in Asia and the United States.

He has served pastorates in Singapore, Indiana, Ohio, and California. He has also preached in Asia, Israel and in over 1,000 churches in the United States.

Patrick received his Doctor of Ministry degree from Fuller Seminary, his Master of Divinity degree from Golden Gate Baptist Seminary (now Gateway Seminary), and his Bachelor of Theology degree from Singapore Bible College. He has Certificates in Non-Profit Management from Stanford University.

Patrick and his wife, Rose, have served God on two continents for forty-five years. They have two adult sons: Joshua is an attorney in San Diego. Jonathan is married to Anna, and they live and work in Ireland. Patrick and Rose are blessed with two adorable grandsons, Josiah and Caleb Pang.

Made in the USA
Middletown, DE
27 November 2024

65521475R00146